MW00834268

A Hard Day's Night

Series Editor: Barry Monush

A Hard Day's Night

Ray Morton

AN IMPRINT OF HAL LEONARD CORPORATION

Copyright © 2011 by Ray Morton

All rights reserved. No part of this book may be reproduced in any form, without written permission, except by a newspaper or magazine reviewer who wishes to quote brief passages in connection with a review.

Published in 2011 by Limelight Editions
An Imprint of Hal Leonard Corporation
7777 West Bluemound Road
Milwaukee, WI 53213

Trade Book Division Editorial Offices
33 Plymouth St., Montclair, NJ 07042

Photo on page 5 of insert © United Artists, courtesy of Photofest. All other photos are from the personal collection of the author.

Printed in the United States of America

Book design by Mark Lerner

Library of Congress Cataloging-in-Publication Data

Morton, Ray, 1961-
 A hard day's night / Ray Morton.
    p. cm. -- (Music on film)
 Includes bibliographical references and index.
 ISBN 978-0-87910-388-0 (pbk.)
 1. Hard day's night (Motion picture) I. Title.
 PN1997.H2593M57 2011
 791.43'72--dc23
                              2011026235

www.limelighteditions.com

To my brother Andrew,
who loves movies and loves the Beatles

CONTENTS

INTRODUCTION

When the Beatles' first feature film, *A Hard Day's Night*, premiered on July 6, 1964, at the very height of Beatlemania, most people in and out of show business assumed it would be a big hit and make lots of money, as everything associated with the Fab Four tended (and still tends) to do. However, few thought that it would actually be a good movie. There was no reason to expect it to be: the picture was a low-budget, black-and-white quickie shot in six short weeks and rushed into release for the sole purpose of serving as an extended advertisement for an accompanying soundtrack album, which United Artists, the film's distributor, hoped would earn its record division a hefty profit before the Beatle craze fizzled out (as everyone, including the Beatles themselves, assumed it eventually would). As long as *A Hard Day's Night* featured enough close-ups of John, Paul, George, and Ringo and showcased a sufficient number of songs, it didn't have to be good. However, it *was* good—so good that it prompted critic Andrew Sarris to famously hail it as "the *Citizen Kane* of jukebox musicals"—and the movie's reputation has continued to grow in the five decades since its release, to the point where it is now considered a bona fide motion picture classic.

What makes *A Hard Day's Night* such a memorable film?

To begin with, it perfectly captures a moment in time— that strange, exciting period so long ago when the world went crazy for four charismatic lads from the north of England whose exhilarating music and vibrant personalities gave people who were still struggling to recover from war, scandal, and assassination something to feel good about. *A Hard Day's Night* documented all the major touchstones of Beatlemania: the adoring hordes that pursued the band members everywhere they went; the hysterical concert audiences whose screams drowned out the very songs they had ostensibly come to hear; the press conferences in which the Beatles bewitched and occasionally bemused the members of the fourth estate; the commercial establishment that sought to exploit the band's appeal without really understanding it; and the harrumphing disgust of an older generation that simply couldn't fathom what all the fuss was about. It also captured the essence of the experience of the four young men at the heart of the phenomenon: how their world was reduced to a seemingly endless string of trains, cars, hotels, and theaters; how they were forced to exist within the confines of a protective (and sometimes imprisoning) cocoon made up of agents, managers, and handlers; how they relied on humor and friendship to get by; and how, no matter how pressured and insane things became, they could always attain joyful release by playing their songs.

In addition, *A Hard Day's Night* created the public face of the Beatles. By most accounts, all four members of the band had remarkably similar personalities, so, in order to differentiate them onscreen, the filmmakers divvied up their joint characteristics and assigned specific traits to each Beatle. Because of the film's great success, these constructed personalities became ingrained in the public's mind, so John Lennon became forever known as an irreverent, sharp-tongued wit; Paul McCartney as an attractive, dashing romantic; George Harrison as a quiet curmudgeon; and Ringo Starr as a loveable sad sack. The film also persuaded the world that the Beatles spent their days joined at the hip; spoke in an endless stream of clever one-liners; and frequently jumped about in pixilated fast motion.

The film also generated some wonderful music. *A Hard Day's Night* introduced six new Beatles songs ("A Hard Day's Night," "I Should Have Known Better," "If I Fell," "And I Love

Her," "Tell Me Why," and "I'm Happy Just to Dance with You"). All six were expertly crafted examples of John Lennon and Paul McCartney's impressive songwriting skills and the band's extraordinary ability to transform these compositions into infectious pop jewels. The title song won a Grammy (for Best Performance by a Vocal Group) and is considered one of the group's true masterpieces, while the other five are standout additions to its remarkable oeuvre.

Finally, *A Hard Day's Night* is so well thought of because it's a great film. It has a simple but intriguing story that gives us a fascinating (if idealized) backstage look at four of the biggest pop-culture icons of all time and the world they inhabited at the pinnacle of their extraordinary success. It's very funny: every one of the film's eighty-seven minutes is filled with humor—sly satire, witty banter, and clever sight gags. Mixed in with the comedy are bits of wistful melancholy that give the film an unexpected but very welcome emotional punch. The film is extremely well made: the acting is good—the Beatles do a more-than-adequate job of playing themselves, and all of the supporting players deliver consistently sharp turns—and the cinematography, production design, costume work, and editing are all quite impressive, especially given how low the budget was and how limited the resources were. Finally, Richard Lester's direction is extraordinary: his affection for the Beatles informs every frame of the movie; his delightfully offbeat sense of humor greatly enhances the onscreen antics; his unique approach to filming the musical numbers was groundbreaking and highly influential; and his playfully innovative use of cinematic techniques such as fast and slow motion, handheld camera, zoom shots, and jump cutting gives the film a wonderfully kinetic energy and spirit that prove to be the perfect visual accompaniment to the Beatles' buoyant sounds.

This is the story of how *A Hard Day's Night* was made.

A Hard Day's Night

CHAPTER 1

Meet the Beatles

The greatest pop music band in history began life as a skiffle group called the Quarrymen in Woolton, a middle-class suburb of Liverpool, England, in March 1957.

Skiffle is a genre of music in which folk, jazz, and blues songs are played on cheap guitars, banjos, and homemade instruments such as washboards and basses fashioned from tea chests. In 1956, an English performer named Lonnie Donegan released a skiffle version of the American folk tune "Rock Island Line." It was a big hit and sparked a skiffle craze in the UK. Within a few short months, thousands of amateur bands had popped up all around the country.

Sixteen-year-old Wooltonite John Lennon got caught up in the excitement. Already a fan of Elvis and rock 'n' roll, John persuaded Mimi Smith, his aunt and guardian, to buy him a guitar and then recruited classmates from the Quarry Bank Grammar School to join him in a group named after their school. Playing covers of established hits, the Quarrymen performed in a number of skiffle contests and at parties, cinemas, and school dances. In July 1957, Ivan Vaughn, the Quarrymen's sometime bass player, invited his friend Paul McCartney to come see the group play at a village fête. Like John, the fifteen-year-old Paul had been inspired by Lonnie Donegan to learn to play the guitar (left-handed). Impressed by Paul's talent, John asked him to join the band. Inspired by singer/songwriter Buddy Holly, John and Paul began writing their own songs, both separately and together, which were then incorporated into the band's repertoire.

By the fall of 1957, the skiffle craze had faded. Many of the recently formed groups disbanded, but some, like the Quarrymen, carried on by fusing skiffle with rock 'n' roll, doo-wop, R&B, and soul into a unique new guitar-and-drum-dominated genre called Beat Music (a.k.a. British Beat or, in Liverpool, Merseybeat, after the Mersey River that flowed through the heart of the city).

Busy with work, school, and life, many of the Quarrymen's founding members began dropping out of the band. To replace them, Paul recruited a fourteen-year-old schoolmate named George Harrison. Harrison, who had taught himself to play guitar by reading a book, joined the group as lead guitarist, and soon afterward the band changed its name to Johnny and the Moondogs. After the Moondogs' drummer departed in 1958, only Lennon, McCartney, and Harrison remained. Using a succession of guest drummers, they began playing in bars, clubs, and other Liverpool venues. When the band found itself in need of a bass player, John—who by then was attending the Liverpool College of Art—convinced his friend, a talented painter named Stuart Sutcliffe, to use the proceeds from the sale of one of his paintings to buy a bass guitar. Although he could hardly play a note, Sutcliffe joined the Moondogs in January 1960, often performing with his back to the audience so they wouldn't see his lack of skill on the instrument.

Lennon and Sutcliffe often hung out in a coffee bar called the Jacaranda, which was owned by Liverpool entrepreneur Allan Williams. Acting as the group's unofficial manager, Williams landed Johnny and the Moondogs an audition for a gig backing Liverpool rocker Billy Fury. Prior to the audition, the group decided they needed a better name. Inspired by Buddy Holly's band, the Crickets, Stu proposed that they adopt the name of one of the motorcycle gangs in the Marlon Brando film *The Wild One*: the Beetles. Adept at clever, imaginative wordplay, John twisted the word to reflect the type of music they were playing and suggested the Beatles instead. Williams didn't like it and offered Long John and the Silver Beetles as an alternative. Lennon didn't want to be called Long John, but did agree to the Silver Beetles, which was eventually modified to the Silver Beatles. The band didn't get the Fury job, but was instead hired to back singer Johnny Gentle on a two-week tour of Scotland in May 1960.

Several months later, Williams was approached by German impresario Bruno Koschmider, who was looking for several bands to play in the clubs and strip joints that he owned in the Reeperbahn, a seedy nightlife (and red light) district in Hamburg. Williams recommended several Liverpool groups, including the Silver Beatles. However, before they could take the gig, the group needed to find a permanent drummer. Pete Best, the son of the owner of the Casbah Club—a Liverpool coffee bar where Lennon, McCartney, Harrison, and Sutcliffe hung out and occasionally played—had his own drum kit and had occasionally sat in with the band, so they asked him to join them on a permanent basis. At the end of August 1960, the group, which dropped the "Silver" and was now known simply as the Beatles, left for Hamburg.

The Beatles' first performances at Koschmider's Indra Club were rather flat, but spurred on by the rowdy German audiences' demand that they "mak show" (put on a show), the group soon developed a raucous stage act. Shouting and stomping their feet as they played, the boys would make jokes, clown around, fight, drink, smoke, and swear while onstage. Their musicianship, which had been just average in their formative years, became sharper and more accomplished. After the Indra was closed down due to complaints about excessive noise, Koschmider moved the Beatles to one of his other venues, an underground establishment called the Kaiserkeller, where they shared the stage with another Liverpool band, Rory Storm and the Hurricanes.

In their off hours, the Beatles hung out with the Hurricanes and soon became friendly with the group's drummer, Ringo Starr, who sat in with them several times when Pete Best failed to turn up. Born in 1940, Starr, whose real name was Richard Starkey, got his nickname because he wore lots of ornate rings; Starkey was shortened so that his drum solos could be advertised as "Starr Time." Meanwhile, Stu met and fell in love with a hip young photography student named Astrid Kirchherr, who took dramatic black-and-white pictures of the Beatles and designed fashionable black leather clothes for them. She also persuaded the boys to cut their hair in a style then all the rage among young continental "Exis" (for Existentialists): long locks brushed down over the forehead, which later became known as the famous Beatle "mop top."

The Beatles left Hamburg after the authorities discovered that seventeen-year-old George Harrison was too young to work in nightclubs (the legal age was eighteen). They returned in April 1961 to play an engagement at an establishment called the Top Ten Club. During this period, a German record producer named Bert Kaempfert hired the boys to serve as the backup band for Liverpool singer Tony Sheridan on a rock version of the Scottish folk song "My Bonnie." Credited to Tony Sheridan and The Beat Brothers, the single was released in Germany on Polydor Records in October and reached number thirty-two on the German charts. When the Top Ten gig came to an end, Stu Sutcliffe decided to remain in Germany to study art and marry Astrid. But before he and Kirchherr could wed, Sutcliffe died of a brain aneurysm on April 10, 1962.

Returning to Liverpool, the Beatles landed a gig playing a lunchtime show at a local joint called the Cavern Club, where the energetic performing style that they had honed in Hamburg became extremely popular. After they received a rave review in *Mersey Beat*, a local music paper, their performances began selling out on a regular basis. When word got out that the group had made a record, their growing legion of fans began asking for it in record shops. The biggest such store in Liverpool was the NEMS (North End Music Stores) on Whitechapel Street, just a few hundred yards from the Cavern Club. When his customers began clamoring for "My Bonnie" by the Beatles, the store's twenty-seven-year-old proprietor, Brian Epstein, tried to order it but could find no trace of either the group or the record in any of his catalogues. When Epstein learned that the Beatles were a local group currently performing nearby, he went down to the Cavern Club to inquire about the single and was immediately captivated by the band's energetic show. Feeling the group had enormous promise, Epstein offered to manage them and they accepted. Epstein's influence on the Beatles was immediate. He spruced up their look by ordering them to stop dressing in jeans and leather and to begin wearing matching suits when performing. Epstein also insisted that the group behave more professionally by being on time, playing to a predetermined set list, and ceasing to roughhouse on stage. He began securing better bookings in higher-class venues and getting them favorable exposure in the press.

Late in 1961, Epstein set out to land the band a recording contract. Since NEMS was one of their biggest customers, the major UK labels were responsive to Epstein's requests that they consider his new discoveries. The Beatles did their first audition, for Decca Records, on New Year's Day 1962. Decca rejected them, insisting that "Guitar groups are on the way out," and the rest of the big record companies soon followed suit. In April 1962, Epstein was referred to George Martin, the head of Parlophone, one of several labels owned by British electronics giant EMI. At the time, Parlophone was a minor label that recorded primarily jazz, spoken word, and comedy acts and had no headliners or consistent big sellers. Hoping to elevate the company's status, Martin was looking for a pop act that could dependably generate hit after hit the way English rock star Cliff Richard ("the British Elvis") and his band the Shadows did for Parlophone's sister label, Columbia. For this reason, Martin agreed to audition the Beatles in June. The producer was impressed with the band members' dynamic personalities and energetic performing style. Martin was also taken with their multiple harmonies, a sound not found in rock music at the time, and with the fact that they performed as a group (with the band members taking turns singing the lead vocals) rather than just as a front man and backing band, which was the usual pop-group configuration of the day. Convinced that the Beatles had strong star potential, Martin signed them to a record contract in July 1962.

The initial plan was to record and release several singles and see how the public would respond. Martin told Brian Epstein that he did not want to use Pete Best on the recordings because he didn't think Best's drumming was very good. The other Beatles had been unhappy with Best's performance for some time and when they heard of Martin's dissatisfaction, they decided to replace him with Ringo Starr, a move they had been contemplating since Hamburg. At first this personnel change created an uproar among the band's

Liverpool fans, many of whom were loyal to Best, but they soon embraced Starr.

The newly reconstituted Beatles had their first official Parlophone recording session on September 4, 1962, during which they performed a mix of their own songs and material written by professional songwriters. Martin wanted to release "How Do You Do It?" by Mitch Murray as the band's first single, but Lennon and McCartney persuaded him to go with one of their original pieces instead. "Love Me Do" was released in October 1962, with "P.S. I Love You" on the B-side. It did moderately well, peaking at number seventeen on the UK singles chart. However, the band's second single, the January 1963 release "Please Please Me" (b/w "Ask Me Why"), did much, much better—making it all the way to number one. The group's first album, also called *Please Please Me* (a studio rendition of the Beatles' stage act recorded in a single day) was released in March 1963 and became a smash hit—it went to number one on the British album charts and remained there for thirty weeks. Released in April, the band's third single, "From Me to You" (b/w "Thank You Girl"), also reached the top spot. The Beatles had arrived.

To promote their records, the band toured the UK three times between February and June, played numerous one-off shows, and began appearing on radio and television. As Liverpool audiences had done, teenagers all over Britain embraced the group and its happy, energetic sound, and soon a wave of what was dubbed "Beatlemania" began sweeping the land. Everywhere the boys went, they were greeted by crowds of adoring fans, and the police frequently had to be called in to keep order. Those same fans began screaming their way through the group's concerts and affectionately pelting the band with Jelly Babies (George Harrison's favorite candy). Before long, the media took notice and began chasing the Beatles with equal fervor. During press conferences and interviews, John, Paul, George, and Ringo displayed an irreverent attitude and cheeky sense of humor that made them even more attractive. Many adults initially disapproved of the Beatles, feeling that their music was nothing but noise and that their long hair and unconventional manner would be a negative influence on the young, but soon their optimistic enthusiasm—which came as a welcome shot in the arm to a country that was still struggling to recover from World War II and had been demoralized by the Suez and Profumo scandals—began winning over grown-ups as well as teens. The sense of sheer possibility that the Beatles represented was also a key part of their appeal—England at that time was still controlled by a very rigid class system, yet here were four middle- and working-class lads breaking out and making it to the top.

The Beatles' upward trajectory continued throughout the summer and fall of 1963. In August, the band's fourth single, "She Loves You," became the fastest-selling record in UK history. On October 13, the boys performed on *Sunday Night at the London Palladium*, England's most popular television show. On November 4, they appeared at the Royal Command Performance. It was during this event that John Lennon famously asked for "the people in the cheaper seats (to) clap your hands. And the rest of you, if you'd just rattle your jewelry. . . ," a good-natured jibe that even the Queen Mother appeared to enjoy. The group's next album, *With the Beatles*, was released on November 22 and went immediately to number one, a spot it held for twenty-one weeks.

As the Beatles' popularity grew, they began receiving offers to do films. This was not unusual: pop stars had been appearing in movies since the beginning of the sound era. From Al Jolson, Rudy Vallée, and Bing Crosby in the 1920s and 1930s to Frank Sinatra in the 1940s and Pat Boone and Doris Day in the 1950s, film producers were eager to cast musical celebrities in the hope that their fans would buy as many movie tickets as they did records. Would the Fab Four be able to repeat their recording success on the silver screen? They, and the world, were about to find out.

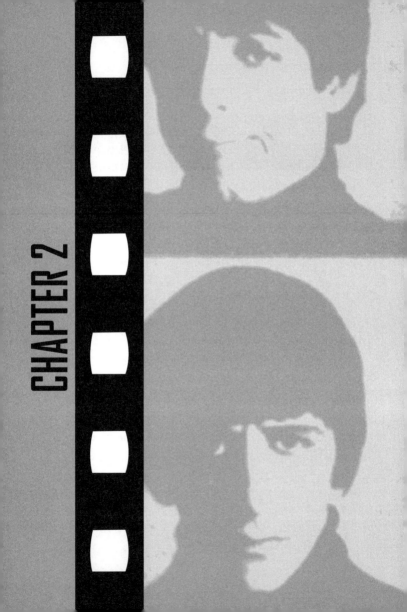

CHAPTER 2

They're Gonna Put Me in the Movies

One of the first film offers the Beatles received was to do a cameo in a movie called *The Yellow Teddy Bears,* a lurid drama about teen sex and pregnancy set in an all-girls school in the English suburbs. The boys were asked to play a band that backs up one of the film's male characters, who dreams of being a pop star. Because director Robert Hartford-Davis wanted to write all the music the Beatles were meant to play in the film himself, they declined (another Beat group called the Embers took their place). British filmmaker Michael Winner, who had recently helmed a musical called *Play It Cool* starring Billy Fury, also wanted to make a movie with the lads. However, by the time he approached Brian Epstein, the Beatles' manager was already deep in negotiations with a major Hollywood film company.

In the wake of the group's incredible success, every music company in the business wanted to make a record with them. However, the exclusive contract that the band had with Parlophone and its parent company, EMI, precluded that. Or so it seemed. Sometime in the late summer or early autumn of 1963, Noel Rodgers, a music publishing executive in the London office of United Artists Records, discovered what appeared to be a loophole in the Beatles' seemingly ironclad agreement with Parlophone. While the contract stated explicitly that the group was bound to the EMI label for original singles and LPs, it made no mention at all of motion picture soundtrack albums. Assuming that if the contract didn't mention something, it didn't cover it, Rodgers reasoned that if the Beatles were to produce a soundtrack album, they were free to make a deal with a company other than Parlophone to release it.

Of course, to make a movie soundtrack album, the Beatles would first have to make a movie. Luckily, United Artists Records was in a unique position to exploit this loophole, because it was a subsidiary of United Artists, the legendary film company started in 1919 by Mary Pickford, Douglas Fairbanks, D. W. Griffith, and Charlie Chaplin and since responsible for great pictures such as *The African Queen*,

High Noon, and *Some Like It Hot*. If United Artists put out a Beatles movie, then UAR could release the soundtrack. Hoping to make this happen, Rodgers approached George "Bud" Ornstein, the executive who ran United Artists' European division, to see if he was interested. Since Beatlemania was at that point primarily a British phenomenon, it wasn't clear if a movie starring the Fab Four would have much of an audience outside of the UK. However, Ornstein figured that if the picture could be made for a low enough price, it could still be profitable, and even if it wasn't, the proceeds from the soundtrack album would almost certainly be significant enough to make the project worth doing. So yes, he was interested.

The proposal was presented to David V. Picker, United Artists' New York-based head of production. Picker, then thirty-two, was a third-generation film industry veteran (his grandfather and father both worked for Loews, Inc., and his uncle, Arnold M. Picker, was the chairman of UA's executive committee) who had been instrumental in bringing movies such as *Tom Jones* and the James Bond series to the company. Although Picker had never heard of the Beatles, he approved Rodgers and Ornstein's idea and gave Ornstein permission to make a three-picture deal (for one film to start and two follow-ups if the first movie was successful) with the band, as long as soundtrack and song-publishing rights for any music created for the film were included.

Ornstein met with Brian Epstein and presented United Artists' offer. Epstein took the proposal to Lennon, McCartney, Harrison, and Starr. The boys were receptive, so Epstein got back to Ornstein and accepted. With the Beatles on board, the studio now had to find someone to actually make the initial film. Picker—who by now had familiarized himself with the group—already knew whom he wanted to direct it: an expatriate American filmmaker living in London named Richard Lester.

Born in Philadelphia on January 19, 1932, Lester was a child prodigy who entered the University of Pennsylvania at the age of fifteen to study clinical psychology. A self-taught musician, Lester helped put himself through school by playing piano in a bar and performing in a vocal group that sang back-up for singer Ginny Stevens on her television program, which was broadcast from WCAU, the CBS affiliate in Philadelphia. After graduating from college in 1951, Lester opted to purse a career in show business and got a job as a stagehand at WCAU. Moving quickly up the ranks, he soon began directing live television programs for the station, but after two years he grew bored, quit his job, and set out for Europe. Lester traveled the continent before heading to London, where he hoped to find backing for a musical that he had written. When none was forthcoming, he found employment as a director for England's new Associated Rediffusion Television (ARTV) network and decided to remain in Britain.

In 1955, Lester was given the opportunity to star in his own series, a variety show spoof called *The Dick Lester Show*. Due to a number of snafus, the first broadcast was a disaster: it earned terrible reviews and the series was immediately canceled. The next day, Lester got a call from Peter Sellers. "I watched your program last night," the comedian told Lester, "and it was either one of the worst shows I've ever seen, or you are on to something." At the time, Sellers was a member (along with Spike Milligan, Harry Secombe, and Michael Bentine) of the cast of *The Goon Show*, an extremely popular British radio program known for its brilliantly absurd and surrealist comedy. The Goons were about to make the transition to television and hired Lester to direct the show. Lester had an offbeat, highly visual sense of humor that meshed well with the Goons' lunatic perspective, and the team went on to make three very successful series—*The Idiot Weekly, Price 2d*; *A Show Called Fred*; and *Son of Fred*—together.

Lester first became interested in moviemaking when he shot several short film sequences for the Goon series. He began frequenting London's National Film Theater and became enamored with the brilliant visual humor of the great silent film comedian Buster Keaton. He also became a fan of the work of François Truffaut, Jean-Luc Godard, and the other members of the burgeoning French New Wave movement—a group of young filmmakers who exploded the conventions of traditional, studio-bound cinema by taking to the streets to make lively, provocative low-budget films filled with unconventional camerawork and innovative editing. Both Keaton and the Nouvelle Vague would prove to be major influences on Lester's later work.

Lester got his first significant celluloid experience when he directed several episodes of the *Mark Saber* television series, but his big breakthrough came in 1959, when he, Peter Sellers, and Spike Milligan used Sellers' new 16-mm home movie camera to make an eleven-minute series of madcap skits, jokes, and sight gags called *The Running Jumping & Standing Still Film*. Blown up to 35 mm and featuring a jazz score composed by Lester himself, the movie was released theatrically in 1960 and received an Academy Award nomination for Best Short Subject.

Following *Running*, Lester directed several documentaries and a string of humorous television commercials that gave him the opportunity to develop and hone an impressive talent for creating comedy on celluloid through clever staging, inventive cinematography, and playful cutting. In 1962, he made his first feature: a low-budget musical about the then-popular traditional jazz scene called *It's Trad, Dad* (a.k.a. *Ring-a-Ding Rhythm!*) that he filled with a wacky, surreal sight gags. On Peter Sellers' recommendation, Lester was then hired to direct 1963's *The Mouse on the Moon*, a sequel to Sellers' 1959 hit *The Mouse That Roared*, a comedy about a small European duchy called Grand Fenwick that declares war on the United States. *The Mouse on the Moon,* in which Grand Fenwick enters the Space Race, was released by United Artists, and brought Lester and David Picker together professionally for the first time. Picker was impressed by Lester's work, especially *The Running Jumping & Standing Still Film*, which had a fresh, original visual style and wonderfully silly spirit that Picker felt would be ideal for the Beatles' cinematic debut.

The film was also going to need a producer, because, unlike the other major studios at that time, United Artists did not make its own movies but instead served as a financier and distributor for independent producers. After a producer developed a project—had a script written and lined up a director, cast, and crew—he would present the package to UA. If the company liked it, it would provide the funds necessary to make the movie and then distribute the final product to theaters, accompanied by the requisite advertising and promotion, in exchange for a significant share (usually 50 percent) of the proceeds. So Picker and Ornstein needed someone to put the Beatle picture together and shepherd it through the production process. Since they wanted Richard Lester to direct the film, they decided to approach someone Lester had already proven he could work effectively with: *The Mouse on the Moon*'s producer, Walter Shenson.

Born in San Francisco in 1918 and educated at Stanford, Shenson began his Hollywood career as a producer and writer of promotional shorts and later became a unit publicist on films such as *From Here to Eternity* and *The Caine Mutiny*. He moved to England in the mid-1950s to become the head of publicity for Columbia Pictures' European division before leaving later in the decade to become a London-based independent producer. His first production was *The Mouse That Roared*, which he followed with *A Matter of WHO*, starring Terry-Thomas, and *The Mouse on the Moon*. All of Shenson's films were made on tight schedules for little money, so he was an ideal choice to supervise the low-budget vehicle that UA envisioned for the Fab Four.

Bud Ornstein got the ball rolling by calling Shenson and asking him to produce a movie for United Artists starring the Beatles and helmed by Richard Lester. Shenson's initial response was to decline—he knew the Beatles' music because his teenage children played it constantly ("Driving me crazy," as Shenson would recall), but he didn't much like it. Ornstein persisted, however, and Shenson—no doubt enticed by the prospect of a definite "go" picture—finally agreed. He was visiting Los Angeles when he received Ornstein's call, so he immediately returned to England and met with Lester at the coffee shop in the London Hilton. Although primarily a jazz aficionado, Lester was familiar with the Beatles, having been introduced to their music by some friends who were Mersey-beat fans. He thought they were terrific and welcomed the chance to make a film with them.

The two men now had to sell themselves to the Beatles, who had the right to approve their collaborators on the film. Shenson met with Brian Epstein to introduce himself, after which a get-together was arranged among Shenson, Epstein, and the Beatles, to take place in Shenson's office. On the appointed day and time, Epstein arrived without the band. He apologized, explaining that the boys had forgotten about the appointment and had instead made plans to go to Abbey Road Studios to watch Gerry and the Pacemakers record some songs that John and Paul had written for them. Shenson still wanted to meet with them, so he and Epstein hailed a taxi and headed for Abbey Road. Along the way, they decided to stop at the Mayfair flat where the band members stayed when they were in London (they would soon move permanently to the capital city from Liverpool) to see if they could catch the boys before they left. The cab pulled up just as the Beatles were coming out of the flat. Not wanting to let the group get away, Shenson offered to give them a ride to the studio.

The Beatles jumped into the cab and during the trip to Abbey Road, the producer "found myself in the middle of a Marx Brothers movie." To begin with, there were six people jammed into a taxi designed for four, so a lot of comical re-arranging was necessary to get everyone settled. During the trip, the Fab Four kept up a constant stream of their charac-teristically humorous patter and every time the cab stopped at a light, one of them would jump out and buy newspapers with Beatles headlines on them. In the midst of all this chaos, Shenson was charmed by the boys' personalities—he found them to be sweet and likable and to have the "same natural humor and wholesomeness as the great movie comedians." Shenson felt that the Beatles were "something very special, on the level of a Keaton or a Fields."

As soon as they arrived at the studio, the band members jumped out of the cab and disappeared inside. An exasper-ated Epstein told Shenson that if he wanted to meet with the Beatles, he was going to have to round them up him-self. "So I found an empty office," Shenson recalled, "and said, 'All right, I'm a very important Hollywood producer, you guys. If you want to make a movie, follow me.' They all said 'Yes sir! Yes sir! Yes sir!'" Once Shenson had the group ensconced, John began the meeting by asking the producer what sort of movie he wanted to make with them. "I don't know," Shenson replied, but following that crazy cab ride, he knew "it should be a comedy." The lads were receptive to this idea and asked who was going to direct. The name Richard Lester was unfamiliar to them, but when Shenson explained that Lester had worked with the Goons (of whom the Beatles were enormous fans) and had directed *The Running Jumping & Standing Still Film* (which they had loved), that was good enough for them. "Okay," John told Shenson after conferring with his bandmates. "You can be the producer."

On October 16, 1963, Shenson brought Richard Lester to meet the Beatles at the BBC Playhouse Theater on Northumberland Avenue, where the group was rehearsing a radio show. The boys took to Lester immediately and the five of them bonded over their mutual love of music and shared quirky sense of humor. By the end of the meeting, the Beatles had approved Lester and the film was a go.

In late October, the band embarked on a five-day tour of Sweden, their first trip abroad since the advent of Beatlemania. While they were gone, Ornstein and Epstein negotiated the fine points of their deal. Prepared to offer the Beatles as much as 25 percent of the film's profits and worried that they were going to want a lot more, Ornstein was stunned when Epstein asked for only 7.5 percent (the lowball request was attributed to the fact that Epstein's only prior experience had been with record royalties, which at the time were relatively small when compared to film profits). Unable to believe his good fortune, Ornstein quickly accepted and negotiated a contract with Epstein that also gave the band a salary of £20,000 (with built-in escalators in both fees and percentages for the other two films in the deal). In exchange, the Beatles agreed to record a batch of new songs for the movie, split the publishing rights to those songs with United Artists Records, and allow UAR to issue the soundtrack.

The studio also worked out a formal arrangement with Walter Shenson. It was agreed that Shenson would produce the movie through his company, Proscenium Films, Ltd. (which would own the film's copyright). United Artists would finance the movie and distribute it. Shenson would receive a £12,000 fee for his producing services and Proscenium would receive half of the film's profits; UA would receive the other half, out of which it would pay the Beatles their 7.5 percent.

During these negotiations, Proscenium's lawyer asked the studio for an unusual concession. In its deals with producers, United Artists normally retained the right to distribute the films that it financed in perpetuity. This made sense, since collecting distribution fees was how the company made its money. However, Walter Shenson had allegedly discovered that UA's 1964 contract with Woodfall Films—the renowned

British production company responsible for movies such as *Tom Jones*, *Look Back in Anger*, and *Saturday Night and Sunday Morning*—contained a special clause that stipulated that the distribution rights to Woodfall's movies would revert to the production company fifteen years after the films were released. Shenson's attorney requested that the same clause be included in Proscenium's contract.

Woodfall had been granted this novel deal point because it had—with *Tom Jones*—produced an Academy Award-winning box office smash, which gave it the prestige and clout to make such a request and United Artists, eager to continue its lucrative relationship with the company, justification for granting it. With only three modest comedies to its credit, Proscenium was hardly in the same league. However, UA's lawyers acceded to the company's request and included the fifteen-year clause in Proscenium's contract. In practical terms, this meant that, come 1979, UA would turn over its half-interest in the Beatles movie to Walter Shenson, who would then control 100 percent of the film's rights and profits.

How UA came to approve such a shortsighted (from the studio's point of view) deal is unknown. Some UA executives familiar with the situation have speculated that the company's lawyers were under the impression that Proscenium was more crucial to the project than it actually was—that they may have thought that Shenson had brought the Beatles to United Artists rather than the other way around—and, knowing how important the film was to the company, agreed to the concession to ensure that the deal went through. David Picker did not find out about any of this until after the contracts had been signed. When he learned that his company's attorneys had given away such a valuable asset—to a producer whom the studio itself had brought into the project—he was furious. However, short of firing the entire legal department (a step he has humorously stated he was tempted to take) there wasn't much he could do about it. Fortunately for the company, United Artists Records retained all of its rights to the movie's sure-to-be-lucrative soundtrack album.

Once his deal was set, Shenson set about assembling the personnel and elements necessary to make the movie. He began by formally hiring Richard Lester to direct the picture for a flat fee of £6,000. Although this was a perfectly adequate salary for such a job, some people connected with the project felt that—since his association with Lester was the only reason Shenson had been asked to produce the film in the first place (and David Picker has stated unequivocally that had Lester declined to direct the picture, Shenson would have definitely been off the project because Picker would have gone in a completely different creative direction with a completely different director/producer team)—Shenson should have given Lester a substantial portion of the profits as well. Lester did not find out about his lynchpin status until many years after the film was made. Whether Shenson knew that Lester was the key to the movie as far as UA was concerned and hid this fact from the director in order to preserve his own creative and financial position on the project or was equally unaware is unknown.

Once Lester was on board, David Picker gave him a free hand to develop the project—he could choose the concept he wanted, the writer he wanted, the creative team he wanted. "I trusted Dick," Picker states.

A budget of £180,000 (approximately $500,000) was established for the production, which was pretty low, even for a low-budget picture. Assuming that the Beatles would be a fleeting phenomenon, Picker and Ornstein wanted to get the movie into theaters as soon as possible, before interest in the group faded. Because the band was booked solid through the end of February 1964, shooting was scheduled to start at the beginning of March, with the film's release set for July 1964.

So the Beatles were going to make a movie. The only question now was: what kind of movie would it be?

CHAPTER 3

It Took Me Weeks to Write

The Beatles certainly knew what sort of a movie they *didn't* want to make.

When rock 'n' roll became big in the 1950s, the film industry was quick to cash in. Hollywood jumped on the bandwagon with the high-profile Elvis Presley movies and exploitation fare such as *Rock Around the Clock* and *Don't Knock the Rock* (both starring Bill Haley and His Comets). In England, rock led to the rise of what came to be known as the "pop musical." Starring innocuous, sanitized rockers such as Cliff Richard (*The Young Ones*, *Summer Holiday*) and Tommy Steele (*The Tommy Steele Story*, *It's All Happening*), these low-budget programs usually featured one of three basic plots: a star is born (fictitious chronicles of how the featured performers hit it big);

"Hey kids, let's put on a show" (in which the star stages a benefit performance to save a beloved landmark or to show disapproving adults that rock music is really good, clean fun); or the road movie (in which the star travels to some exotic location, meets girls, and sings songs). Pop musicals were contrived, formulaic, and filled with corny romances and kitschy song-and-dance numbers created by people with little feel for or understanding of rock 'n' roll. The Beatles loathed these films and didn't want to appear in one. "Never mind all your pals," John Lennon said, "how could we have faced each other if we had allowed ourselves to be involved in that kind of movie?"

They didn't have to worry—Richard Lester and Walter Shenson didn't want to make a pop musical either. Rather than force the Fab Four into some silly, inconsequential plot, Lester and Shenson thought the subject of the movie should be the Beatles themselves. Why ask John, Paul, George, and Ringo to play fictitious characters when their own personalities were so much more vibrant and interesting than any that could be concocted? (Besides, given the group members' collective lack of acting experience, it seemed unlikely that they could successfully play anyone other than themselves anyway.) Likewise, it seemed a waste to involve the band in a fictitious narrative when their real-life escapades were as exciting as any made-up adventure could ever be. A straight documentary would have been too dry, so Lester and Shenson decided instead to make what the director called a "fictionalized documentary" that compressed all the group's extraordinary Beatlemania-fueled experiences into a single "typical" day in their lives, exaggerated them for dramatic and comedic effect, and provided plenty of opportunities for the boys to play their music and sing their songs.

In need of a screenwriter to develop this idea further, Lester approached Johnny Speight, creator of the popular British situation comedy *Till Death Us Do Part*. Speight was interested, but prior commitments kept him from participating. After also considering Alan Simpson and Ray Galton, writers of another popular sitcom, *Steptoe and Son,* Lester suggested Alun Owen.

Born in Wales in 1925 but raised in Liverpool, Owen was a former actor whom Lester had directed on *The Dick Lester Show*; *The Idiot Weekly, Price 2d*; and *Son of Fred*. He had since gone on to become a playwright and radio and television scriptwriter who had achieved great success writing about his hometown: *Progress to the Park*, a play about four friends coming of age in Liverpool, was produced both onstage and on the radio, and the teleplay *No Trams to Lime Street*, about three sailors on leave in the port city, had been extremely popular when it aired on England's ITV network in 1959. Lester felt that Owen's familiarity with Liverpool and his ability to write in the city's vernacular would be an asset to the project. Paul McCartney and Brian Epstein, both of whom had seen and very much liked *No Trams to Lime Street*, agreed and persuaded the rest of the band that Owen would be an excellent choice. Unfortunately, the writer was currently working on a new Liverpool-set musical called *Maggie May* with composer Lionel Bart (*Oliver!*) and was unavailable. Moving on, Shenson and Lester interviewed a number of other writers, but, according to Shenson, "they all had terrible, trendy ideas" (one allegedly suggested that the Beatles travel about in a souped-up van filled with James Bond-style gadgets). Fortunately, *Maggie May* was postponed and Alun Owen happily signed on to the project.

As a first step, Owen accompanied the Beatles when they flew to Ireland on November 7, 1963 to play two shows at the Adelphi Cinema. Owen used the three-day trip as an opportunity to get to know the boys—their personalities, their relationships with one another, and their humor. He was struck by the insulated quality of the Beatles' existence: upon their arrival in Dublin, their handlers hustled them from their plane to a car, to their hotel and to the theater, and then back to the hotel and back to the plane. They never had a moment to themselves, and "the only freedom they ever had," Owen recalled, "was when they were onstage playing—then their faces would light up."

By the time Owen returned to London, he had developed a theme for the film that he presented to Lester and Shenson: "[The Beatles] are prisoners of their success. They go from the airport to the hotel to the theater or stadium or concert hall to the hotel back to the airport. In any city, it's always the same. They literally travel in a cocoon of Liverpool. There's the manager, the road manager, a publicity man, the car driver, the guy who carries the equipment. That's all they see, because they'd be mobbed if they got out of the car or out of the hotel room or away from the concert hall." Lester responded enthusiastically to Owen's concept because it echoed a remark that John Lennon had made after the band returned from Sweden that had intrigued the director. When Lester asked John if he had enjoyed the Swedish trip, Lennon's reply was, "Yes, very much. It was a room and a car and a room and a concert and we had cheese sandwiches sent up to the hotel room."

To research this notion, Lester, Owen, and Walter Shenson went along with the Beatles when the band traveled to Paris on January 14, 1964 for a three-week engagement at the Olympia Theater. The filmmakers spent a long weekend with the group and its retinue at the Hotel George V, and as they shared the boys' hermetically sealed existence—taking all their meals from room service, riding around with the lads in their car, accompanying them as they made their way through the screaming crowds, and hanging around with the boys backstage at the Olympia—"a screenplay began to form in our minds," Lester recalled. "The film was writing itself right in front of us . . . because we were watching it happen. It was absolutely on a plate."

Returning to the UK, Lester, Owen, and Shenson devised a simple story line for their film that would chronicle the Beatles' adventures as they travel to London via train to perform on a television program. Lester crafted a structure that he wanted the story to follow. The first third would depict the band's claustrophobic life on the road, leading to a moment when they finally get fed up and escape for a while to enjoy a bit of freedom. The next section would show the group at work—rehearsing for the show, having their wardrobe fitted, getting their makeup done, etc. To add a bit of suspense, the last part of the narrative would introduce a problem that had to be resolved prior to the finale, which would show the boys in concert, performing a selection of their hits.

The trio also came up with a list of other elements that they wanted to incorporate into the narrative:

- As agreed, the Beatles would play themselves—albeit idealized versions of themselves ("Minus," Lester joked, "the swearing, smoking, and sex"). However, because the band members' real-life personalities were so similar,

Lester and Owen wanted to give each one a specific characterization in order to differentiate them onscreen. "We were trying to separate their characters officially," Lester explained, "because they were—especially at this time— more like each other than was safe. And we were desperately trying to give them separate characteristics . . . (so) Paul was the sexy one, John was clever and sarcastic, Ringo was loveable, and George was mean. It was really simple. We set out to produce the same gag that [could] be dealt with over and over, like Jack Benny." In addition, each Beatle would be given a solo scene of his own as a personal showcase.

- Because the Beatles were not actors, Lester wanted Owen to put them into situations they were already used to: "We knew the standard of acting experience, and the more we could give them situations that were familiar to them—like doing a press conference—the better the odds they would be able to carry it off moderately well. They were almost entirely asked to do what they did: go to a club, to go to a rehearsal room, to send up a director."

- Lester wanted to include scenes of the Beatles taking on (in a comedic way) authority figures, the upper class, and people seeking to exploit them in order to highlight what he felt was a key aspect of their importance and their appeal:

The quality of confidence that the boys exuded! Confidence that they could dress as they liked, speak as they liked, talk to the Queen as they liked, talk to people . . . who 'fought the war for them' as they liked. You must accept that this is a film based on a class society . . . a society that was still based on privilege—privilege by schooling, privilege by birth, privilege by accent, privilege by speech. They were the first people to attack this—the Beatles sent the class thing sky-high; they laughed it out of existence and, I think, introduced a tone of equality more successfully than any other single factor that I know. . . . They said if you want to do something, do it. Forget all this talk about . . . money or . . . education or family background. . . . Just do it. And this has been their great strength.

- Drama requires conflict, but since the filmmakers didn't want to show the band members at odds with one another, Owen came up with the idea of having one of the boys bring along a troublemaking grandfather to generate tension and dissension.
- The Beatles' management team would be represented in the film by two fictional characters: road manager Norm—a combination of Brian Epstein and the band's real-life road man, Neil Aspinall—and equipment wrangler/

electrician Shake, who was loosely based on the group's loyal roadie, Mal Evans.

- Because it didn't seem likely that the Beatles would be able to handle long speeches, Lester requested that Owen construct the dialogue primarily in snappy, easy-to-remember one-liners.

- While it was a given that the story needed to provide opportunities for the Beatles to play the music they were composing for the movie, the filmmakers did not want to include the cheesy song-and-dance numbers usually seen in pop musicals. Instead, they wanted to show the Beatles playing only in circumstances in which they would actually perform in real life: in rehearsal, in concert, etc.

- The team also did not want to include any sort of love interest in the story. Lester and the Beatles didn't want one because they thought it would be silly. Walter Shenson was opposed because a friend's teenage daughter told him that the Beatles' female fans didn't want to see any of the boys involved with women onscreen—it would spoil their fantasies of one day being able to date the boys themselves. (This was the reason the fact that John Lennon was married and had a young son was continually downplayed by the band's publicists and would not be mentioned in the film.)

With the basic narrative and conceptual elements decided, Owen set to work on the actual screenplay. He wrote quickly and in a matter of weeks had produced the first draft of a script titled simply *The Beatles*.

Richard Lester had extremely mixed feelings about this initial version. He was pleased with Owen's clever dialogue and with the effective characterizations the writer had developed for the Fab Four. Lester also appreciated the exuberant spirit and generous helping of Liverpudlian whimsy that Owen had infused into the script—especially a bit in which Norm gets mad at Shake for "always being taller than me to spite me," a nonsensical notion that Lester loved. However, the director also felt that the first draft was too long; relied too much on dialogue to tell the story rather than conveying it through action and images (a common problem for many playwrights who write for film); and lacked sufficient visual humor. Much to Owen's displeasure, Lester decreed that the screenplay was going to need an extensive rewrite.

Working together, the writer and director cut down the script, found ways to tell the story pictorially rather than verbally, and incorporated a generous helping of sight gags devised by the director. According to Lester, only one sequence from the initial draft—the train trip that the boys take to London at the beginning of the film—survived relatively intact into the second. Everything else either had been significantly revised or was completely new.

All of this was pretty much par for the course—most screenplays are heavily revised in the transition from rough draft to shooting script. However, coming from the theater and from British television—worlds in which an author usually has total control over his material—Owen found the collaboration difficult. "He [Owen] never had to shape a picture," Lester recalled. "That's where a lot of the arguments came in. Whenever I complained . . . he would throw the script on the floor and sulk and say, 'You tell me what you want and I will do it. I'm paid as a cheap writer.'"

Despite these struggles, Owen eventually produced a much more satisfactory second draft, which was the one Lester would take into production (with Owen remaining on set to provide polishes as necessary). The result of his efforts unfolds as follows:

After eluding a crowd of screaming fans, the Beatles—accompanied by their road manager, Norm, their equipment manager, Shake, and Paul's grandfather, a crafty old coot with a penchant for causing trouble—board a train headed for London, where they are scheduled to give a televised concert. Following an eventful trip in which they put a condescending upper-class businessman in his place, prevent Paul's grandfa-

ther from becoming engaged to a rich lady, and flirt with some pretty girls, the group arrives in the capital city.

After pushing through another crowd and making it safely to their hotel, the boys are instructed to stay in and answer their fan mail. Itching for some fun, they instead decide to sneak out to a nightclub, but are only able to grab a few minutes of relaxation before Norm rounds them up and marches them back to the hotel.

The next morning, they are driven to the television theater to prepare for that evening's broadcast. Upon arrival, they are obliged to participate in a crowded press reception during which they are asked a series of increasingly inane questions. Moving to the stage, the band is ordered about by the program's antagonistic director and his unsympathetic crew as they attempt to rehearse. Fed up with the suffocating environment, the boys duck out a fire exit and escape to an empty field, where they enjoy a few liberating minutes of freedom playing an impromptu game of soccer before being ordered off the grass by the lot's cantankerous owner. Returning to the theater, they continue to prepare for the show by rehearsing a few more songs, getting fitted for wardrobe, and submitting themselves to ministrations of hair and makeup artists.

During a break, Paul's troublemaking grandfather convinces a gullible Ringo that his fellow Beatles are taking advantage of him and that by staying with them he is missing out on life.

Stirred up, Ringo deserts the band and walks out of the theater in a huff. The other Beatles search for him, to no avail.

Ringo wanders the streets and has a few misadventures that finally lead to his getting arrested and taken to the local police station, where he is reunited with Paul's grandfather (who was taken into protective custody after being mobbed by fans while trying to sell pictures of the Beatles upon which he has forged the lads' signatures). Convinced the police are about to work them over, Paul's grandfather decides to escape. Leaving Ringo behind, he runs out of the police station and back to the television theater, and tells the band where their prodigal drummer is. With only a few minutes left to go before show time, John, Paul, and George set out to liberate Ringo from the authorities. They break him out of the police station, the cops come afer them, and a madcap chase ensues.

Arriving back at the theater just in time, the Beatles put on a triumphant concert for an auditorium full of screaming fans. However, there's no time to savor the triumph: minutes after they take their final bow, Norm and Shake load the boys onto a helicopter and whisk them off to their next engagement.

CHAPTER 4

Roll on Up

As the script was taking shape, Richard Lester and Walter Shenson began assembling the filmmaking team that would help them bring *The Beatles* to life.

To handle the practical, nuts-and-bolts aspects of the production—preparing budgets and schedules, ordering equipment, securing filming locations, and hiring crews—Denis O'Dell was brought in to serve as the movie's associate producer. An experienced assistant director and line producer, O'Dell had just returned to England from a long stay in Yugoslavia, where he had supervised the shooting of the Richard Widmark/Sidney Poitier Viking epic *The Long Ships,* when he received a call from Bud Ornstein asking him to join *The Beatles*. Exhausted, O'Dell declined, but when his teenage children discovered that he had turned down a chance to work with their favorite band, they badgered him into calling Ornstein back and accepting. One of O'Dell's first tasks was to establish a production base for the film at Twickenham Film Studios. Located in the London suburb of St. Margarets, the facility would house the movie's sets and offices; costume, makeup, and prop workshops; and editing rooms.

Since *The Beatles* was conceived as a fictional documentary, Lester decided that he wanted the film to look like a real documentary—he felt this would greatly enhance the movie's reality and believability. Adopting the techniques of the French New Wave filmmakers he so admired, Lester planned to shoot the black-and-white production (the budget was too low to afford color film) on as many real locations as possible, using an informal visual style that incorporated a good deal of handheld camera work, liberal use of zoom lenses, and as much natural lighting as possible. For this reason, he recruited veteran British cinematographer Gilbert Taylor (*Dr. Strangelove or: How I Learned to Stop Worrying and Love the Bomb*). Taylor had photographed *It's Trad, Dad* for Lester in a similar fashion and the director wanted him to push the concept further in their new film.

John Jympson, acclaimed for his stellar work on *Zulu*, was engaged to edit the picture and Ray Simm (*Billy Liar*) signed on as art director. *The Beatles* was scheduled to be shot on a mixture of sets and real locations in and around London; it was Simm's job to help select and dress the real-world locales and to design the artificial settings. Lester asked Simm to ensure that as many of the sets as possible—especially in the first half of the film—had low ceilings, in order to subtly emphasize the claustrophobic nature of the Beatles' existence.

The film's costumes would be designed by Julie Harris (*The Chalk Garden*, *Swiss Family Robinson*), working in conjunction with the Beatles' regular tailor, Dougie Millings. Millings had created all the distinctive matching suits the boys had worn onstage since Brian Epstein first ordered them to spruce up their attire. For the movie, he would design new outfits for each Beatle. Five copies would be made of each piece of clothing, both for practical reasons (so that replacements would be on hand if the clothes got damaged or soiled during filming) and because fans kept stealing them.

Other key crew members included: John D. Merriman (first assistant director), Derek V. Browne (camera operator), John O'Gorman (makeup), Betty Glasow (hair), Rita Davison (continuity), H. L. Bird (sound recording), Gordon Daniel (sound editor), and Pamela Tomling and Roy Benson (assistant film editors).

During this period, Lester also began assembling a cast, beginning with the three actors who would support the Beatles throughout the film.

Lester's first choice for the role of Paul's grandfather was Irish actor Dermot Kelly, but when he proved to be unavailable, his fellow Irishman Wilfrid Brambell got the part. Born in Dublin in 1912, Brambell worked as a reporter before becoming a professional actor. He appeared at the Abbey and Gate theaters in Dublin and worked in repertory theaters throughout England, then moved into television in the 1950s, where he specialized in playing old men even though he was only in his forties. In 1962, Brambell began starring as elderly rag-and-bone man Albert Steptoe in the hit sitcom *Steptoe and Son*. In one of the show's running gags, Brambell's character was constantly called a "dirty old man," which inspired Alun Owen to have several characters in *The Beatles* refer to the grandfather as a very clean old man.

The role of Norm, the band's road manager, was given to Liverpool native Norman Rossington (called "Neil" in the original script, the character was renamed for Rossington). Born on December 24, 1928, Rossington was employed as a messenger, carpenter, and draughtsman before he decided to become an actor. After training at the Bristol Old Vic, he moved to London and began working in the theater. He also appeared on the popular sitcom *The Army Game* and in films such as *A Night to Remember*, *Saturday Night and Sunday Morning*, *The Longest Day*, and *Lawrence of Arabia*.

He also made a brief appearance in *The Running Jumping & Standing Still Film*.

John Junkin was cast as Shake, the Beatles' equipment handler. Born on January 29, 1930, Junkin began his career as a radio and television script writer and first met Richard Lester and Alun Owen while writing for *The Idiot's Weekly, Price 2d*. Junkin happened to be on set one day when Lester was rehearsing a fencing segment featuring Owen. When the actor playing opposite Owen fell ill, Lester asked Junkin to fill in. Junkin agreed and thus kicked off a second career as a popular character actor. Born and raised in the London borough of Ealing, he had to affect a scouse (Liverpool accent) for his role as Shake.

As the team moved forward preparing the film for production, something unexpected happened: the Beatles went from being a British phenomenon to a worldwide one. When the project was conceived in the fall of 1963, the band's popularity was confined mostly to the UK. During the preproduction period, they began reaching out to Europe with some success (the Swedes loved them; the French were mostly indifferent), but had yet to make any impact in the United States—the world's biggest, most influential, and therefore most important market.

It wasn't for lack of trying. When "Please Please Me" went to number one in the UK, George Martin asked Capitol

Records, EMI's American subsidiary, to release it in the United States, but Capitol head Alan Livingston refused. No British pop act had ever succeeded in America. Even Cliff Richard, England's biggest rock star, had failed to catch on in the States despite making an extensive tour and charting a respectable number of singles, and Livingston didn't think the Beatles would do any better. A frustrated Martin was forced to make deals with two independent American labels instead. "Please Please Me" and "From Me to You" were released by Chicago-based Vee-Jay Records and "She Loves You" was released by a New York company named Swan Records. Both labels were small and neither had the resources to mount the required large-scale promotional and distribution campaigns, so all three singles failed. It was looking as if the Beatles would never break through in the United States when fate—in the awkward, homely figure of Ed Sullivan—intervened.

Sullivan, the former Broadway columnist whose eponymous CBS Sunday night variety show was the premiere launching pad for new talent in America, was at Heathrow Airport on October 31, 1963, the day the Beatles returned from their tour of Sweden. The boys' plane was met by thousands of screaming fans, and although he had never heard of the band, Sullivan figured that any act capable of generating that much commotion was worth having on his program. A deal was negotiated with Brian Epstein for the Beatles to appear on *The Ed Sullivan Show* three times in February 1964 (twice live and once on tape). The bookings caused Capitol to finally see the light. Realizing that three segments on one of the country's most popular and influential television programs was too good a promotional opportunity to pass up, the record company agreed to release the Beatles' next single.

Capitol's initial plan was to put out "I Want to Hold Your Hand"—which became an instant hit in the UK when it was released there in November 1963—on January 13, 1964, a few weeks in advance of the Beatles' first appearance on the Sullivan show. But in mid-December 1963, *CBS News* did a report on Beatlemania that introduced the group to a wide American audience for the first time. The report included a clip of the band performing "I Want to Hold Your Hand," and large numbers of people began calling radio stations and asking the deejays to play the song. A few stations had copies of the record sent from England and began spinning it ahead of its official issue date, prompting Capitol to move the single's release up to December 26. It was a wise move: "I Want to Hold Your Hand" sold a quarter of a million records in its first three days of availability and would eventually sell over five million copies. On February 1, 1964, the song hit number one on the U.S. charts.

The Beatles flew to America on February 7 and immediately took the country—still reeling from the assassination of President John F. Kennedy and needing something to feel good about—by storm. The band was met at Kennedy Airport by 3,000 screaming fans and mobbed by hundreds more at the Plaza Hotel. Their first live performance on *The Ed Sullivan Show* on February 9, 1964 was watched by 74 million viewers; their second, on February 16, attracted 70 million. They also gave three concerts—one at the Washington Coliseum on February 11 and two at Carnegie Hall on February 12—and all were sellouts. Beatles merchandise flew off the shelves, and the American press covered the boys with the same frenzied enthusiasm as had their British counterparts. Beatlemania had officially arrived in the United States, and from there it quickly spread to the rest of the globe.

None of this escaped the notice of United Artists. Determined to cash in on the band's suddenly expanded popularity, the studio decided that, rather than release the picture gradually in territories across the world (the usual pattern at the time), it would be given a massive, near-simultaneous worldwide launch. To keep the Beatles from jumping ship and accepting one of the other lucrative offers now coming their way, UA voluntarily raised the band's percentage of the film's profits from 7.5 to approximately 20 percent. In addition, the group's salary was bumped to £25,000.

The Beatles returned to the UK from America on February 22, 1964 and on February 25 (George Harrison's twenty-first birthday) joined with producer George Martin to begin recording the songs they had written for the movie: "I Should Have Known Better," "If I Fell," "And I Love Her," "I'm Happy Just to Dance with You," and "Tell Me Why."

All five songs, which were penned mostly during the band's trips to Paris and the United States, were jointly credited to John Lennon and Paul McCartney, like all of the duo's Beatle-era compositions. In truth, while the two did collaborate on some tunes, they wrote the majority of their songs separately (although often with some assistance from the other). "I'm Happy Just to Dance with You" was written by Lennon and McCartney together; "I Should Have Known Better" and "Tell Me Why" were written by Lennon alone; "If I Fell" was written primarily by John, with some help from Paul; "And I Love Her" was penned by McCartney, with some lyrical contributions from Lennon. Following band tradition, the lead vocal for each song was sung by its principal author. The exception was "I'm Happy Just to Dance with You," which was given to George Harrison to perform.

Two songs not written for the movie—"I Call Your Name," which Lennon and McCartney had composed prior to the formation of the Beatles and had previously been recorded by Billy J. Kramer with the Dakotas, and a cover of

Little Richard's "Long Tall Sally," which, as sung in blistering fashion by Paul, had long been a staple of their stage act—were also taped for use in the film. All of the songs were recorded at Abbey Road Studios on four-track EMI British tape recorders (which allowed for the overdubbing of multiple musical layers onto a single track to create a richer sound).

On February 25 the group did three takes of "And I Love Her" and three takes of "I Should Have Known Better." Unhappy with the results, they returned to the studio on Wednesday, February 26, and did sixteen additional takes of "And I Love Her" and eighteen additional takes of "I Should Have Known Better." At this point, they were satisfied with "I Should Have Known Better," but they came back on Thursday, February 27, and did two more takes of "And I Love Her" before finally declaring it finished. Later that same day, they recorded "Tell Me Why" in eight takes and "If I Fell" in fifteen.

On Saturday, February 29, the Beatles met with Richard Lester and Alun Owen to do a read-through of the completed screenplay. The boys were happy with the script, which they (and those who knew them) felt did a good job of capturing their personalities, speech, and sensibilities. Owen and Lester were happy with the deft way the novice actors handled their dialogue: "They just nailed it!" Owen exclaimed.

The band returned to Abbey Road on Sunday, March 1 to record "I'm Happy Just to Dance with You" in four takes.

They then recorded "I Call Your Name" in seven takes and "Long Tall Sally" in one.

Once all the songs were finished and mixed, Richard Lester reviewed them to decide where he would put them in the film. Although the script indicated where musical numbers were to occur in the story, it did not specify which pieces were to be used in those spots. The director selected "I Should Have Known Better" for the scene in which the boys serenade a group of girls they meet on the train. "If I Fell," "And I Love Her," and "I'm Happy Just to Dance with You" were chosen for scenes of the band rehearsing. "Tell Me Why" would be featured (along with reprises of some of the other songs) in the big concert scene that climaxes the movie. It is thought that "Long Tall Sally" was originally intended to be the concert's closing number, since the Beatles had finished all their U.S. shows with it. Ultimately, however, the decision was made to drop "Long Tall Sally" and use the band's signature tune, "She Loves You," instead. "I Call Your Name" was also dropped, and both rejects ended up on the band's next EP, *Long Tall Sally*.

When the March 1 recording session wrapped at 10 p.m., John, Paul, George, and Ringo all went home to get some sleep. They were going to need it, because *The Beatles* was scheduled to start shooting at eight o'clock the following morning.

CHAPTER 5

A Hard Month's Shoot

The Beatles began filming on Monday, March 2, 1964.

As the cameras rolled, Richard Lester had one primary goal: to capture the spirit of the Beatles on celluloid as accurately as possible. "I had a marvelous image in front of me to reflect and that was . . . their energy and their originality. So, you know, all [I] did was to say . . . 'How can I, as a filmmaker, best serve what I find so attractive in these four people?'"

He began by creating a relaxed atmosphere in which the novice actors would feel comfortable: "I worked to make it as light as possible, so that you were not really aware that this was anything serious or important going on. Just keep it on a terribly easy level."

Lester generally kept the camera loose, so the Beatles wouldn't have to worry about hitting precise marks. If one of the boys flubbed a line, the director wouldn't fuss; instead, he just kept shooting and had them repeat the dialogue that had gone awry. If that didn't work, he would simply give them an entirely new line to say.

During the first week of filming, Lester realized that the Beatles never played a scene the same way twice, which wreaked havoc with the film's continuity. To rectify this, he began using two cameras to film every scene, which allowed him to photograph the close-ups and wide angles simultaneously so that the boys wouldn't have to worry about matching their actions precisely from shot to shot. Lester was so happy with the results that this became his standard way of working on all his films from then on. He would occasionally film rehearsals without telling the lads that the cameras were running in order to capture a more laid-back, unguarded performance.

Worried that the Beatles would become self-conscious if they saw themselves onscreen, Lester didn't want them to watch the rushes, so he would screen them in secret during his lunch breaks. The Beatles began to wonder where their director was sneaking off to, and one day they followed him and barged in on the screening. From then on, they joined Lester almost every day.

TOP: The Beatles at the start of their meteoric rise.

LEFT: Director Richard Lester.

TOP: Lester and the boys with producer Walter Shenson.

BOTTOM RIGHT: The Fab Four at work with their record producer, George Martin.

BOTTOM LEFT: Abbey Road Studios, where the Beatles made most of their records and where they first met with Walter Shenson to discuss making a movie.

TOP: *Summer Holiday*: the kind of pop musical that the Beatles didn't want to make.

BOTTOM: The Beatles get primped by the girls from the train sequence: Pattie Boyd attends to George while Prue Bury grooms Paul.

TOP: Filming the "escape" scene on the fake helipad at Isleworth.

RIGHT: John and Millie (Anna Quayle).

TOP: John Junkin and Norman Rossington as Shake and Norm, the Beatles' loyal roadies.

BOTTOM: On the run in Notting Hill Gate.

The one, the only, the fab new novel about those international sensations

DELL
0489
50c

The BEATLES
in
A HARD DAY'S NIGHT

by JOHN BURKE

Now a swinging, gear* movie released by United Artists and starring Ringo, Paul, John and George

plus 8 pages of exclusive photos from the movie

*Translation: the greatest

TOP: The concert scene.

LEFT: To help promote the film, Alun Owen's screenplay was transformed into a paperback novel.

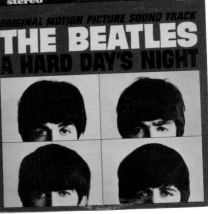

FROM TOP: Parlophone Records' version of the movie's soundtrack album; the United Artists version; Capitol Records' collection of the movie's songs.

A unique, handbill-style poster that was pasted up in towns across America to announce the film's impending release.

While no one would ever accuse the Beatles of being master thespians, Lester's approach gave the lads the room to blossom into captivating screen personalities. When Walter Shenson's wife asked him after the first day of filming if the Beatles could act, he said, "I don't know. But I do know you can't take your eyes off them."

Lester directed the rest of the film in the same loose manner, leaving plenty of room for spontaneity and on-the-spot invention. If a member of the cast or crew came up with an ad lib that Lester liked, he'd use it. If something interesting happened on the set, he would find a way to work it into the scene. If mistakes were made or problems arose, Lester would maneuver around them or else incorporate them into the picture. He reworked scenes and sequences on the spot to make them more effective and frequently tossed in new, unscripted gags at the last minute. In keeping with his absurdist sense of humor, some of these gags were surreal in nature. Although they seemed incongruous with the realistic approach that he had dictated for the picture, Lester wasn't bothered by the apparent discrepancy; for him, the documentary style was a jumping-off point for the film rather than a formal end in itself. Lester felt the absurd gags were justified because they kept the piece fresh and, since this was the sort of humor that the Beatles enjoyed, accurately reflected the band's sensibility.

"I worked instinctively," the director recalled. "I don't preplan anything. . . . I have seen directors who write down a list of scenes for the day and then sit back in a chair while everything is filmed according to plan. I can't do that. I know that good films can be made this way, but it's not for me. I have to react on the spot. I am a butterfly by instinct. My ideal is a few gags, a few situations, and tremendous mobility in between." Lester's "ideal" gave the film a terrific sense of life and vitality.

This vitality was greatly enhanced by the speed at which the movie was made. With only six weeks to produce an entire feature, the cast and crew had to complete dozens of shots every day, often with numerous changes of location. The only way to accomplish this was to work long hours at a frantic pace. Cinematographer Gilbert Taylor—who sometimes had to take Benzedrine to keep going—characterized the entire shoot as a lot of "kick, bollock, and scramble."

All the kicking, bollocking, and scrambling began at London's Paddington Station.

Monday, March 2–Friday, March 6 / Monday, March 9

The first day of filming started with John, Paul, George, and Ringo joining Actor's Equity, the British actors' union. Wilfrid Brambell proposed them for membership and Norman

Rossington seconded the proposal. After being sworn in and receiving their membership cards from the Equity rep, the boys pushed their way through the crowd of fans and reporters that had gathered at the station and boarded a train to begin shooting the traveling-to-London sequence that opens the movie.

These train scenes could have been filmed on a studio set, but Richard Lester preferred to shoot in a real vehicle to enhance the sense of realism he was trying to create. The train was a "special" chartered from British Rail. The railroad's executives only charged the production £600 a day—the basic cost of the vehicle's operation. The executives were willing to give the filmmakers such a good deal in exchange for some photos of the Beatles riding on the train that could be used for promotional purposes (some of the executives also requested a few autographed pictures for themselves). For six days, the special left Paddington every morning at 8 a.m., traveled under escort to the west coast of England, then turned around and headed back to London.

At the end of the first day of shooting, the Beatles decided to avoid the crowd at Paddington and got off the train at the suburban Acton Main Line station instead. This proved to be a wise decision, because when the company arrived back in London, a young camera assistant named Peter Ewens emerged from the train carrying the cans of film that had been shot that day. Ewens had a mop-top haircut, and when the crowd that was awaiting the Fab Four's return saw him, they mistook him for a Beatle and chased after him. As he ran for his life, the terrified Ewens dropped a few of the film cans, which popped open and exposed some valuable footage to the light. From then on, the Beatles avoided Paddington completely by both embarking and disembarking at Acton Main Line and other suburban stations.

Initially the movie train traveled to the coastal town of Minehead in Somerset, but so many fans turned up along the route that after three days the destination was changed to nearby Taunton and then to Newton Abbot. These switches were supposed to be secret, but somehow word got out and the fans continued to line the sidings.

The first part to be filmed on board the train was the dining car scene, in which Paul's grandfather tries to drive a wedge between Norm and Shake while the Beatles flirt with some schoolgirls, played by models Prue Bury and Pattie Boyd, whom Lester cast after directing her in a potato chip commercial. During the shoot, Boyd and George Harrison took a liking to each other. They soon began dating and eventually married.

The second major sequence to be shot on the rails was the one in which John, George, and Ringo (and later Norm and Shake) meet Paul's grandfather in one of the train's passenger compartments. As the scene continues, Grandfather departs with Norm and Shake and the Beatles get into a battle of wills with a condescending upper-class businessman (played by character actor Richard Vernon, soon to appear as the head of the Bank of England in *Goldfinger*) who attempts to take over the compartment. The businessman's actions lead to one of the movie's most famous lines: after the haughty gentleman complains to the lads that he "fought the war for your sort," Ringo responds with, "Bet you're sorry you won!"

Lester injected the film's first bit of surrealism into the end of this scene: as the Beatles leave the compartment, they make faces at the businessman. Turning away, the man looks out the window and is surprised to see the boys suddenly appear outside the train, running alongside the moving carriage yelling, "Hey mister, can we have our ball back?" The shot was created by photographing the Beatles as they jogged along the platform next to the slow-moving vehicle at the Crowcombe station in Somerset.

Also photographed during the company's week in transit were scenes of the Beatles invading a compartment full of girls, Ringo flirting wistfully with a beautiful woman, and Paul preventing Grandfather from becoming engaged to a rich lady.

Shooting on the train wasn't easy:

- There wasn't enough electricity, so the company had to install a five-kilowatt generator in one of the carriages to power all its equipment.

- Space was at a premium, so most of the sequences were shot with a handheld camera because the train's corridors and compartments were too cramped and narrow to accommodate dollies and tripods.

- Although all of the scenes were shot with synchronous sound, there was so little room that the unit could not use a camera equipped with a sound blimp (a shell that fits around the camera to muffle the noise of its motor). Since the camera's grinding could be heard on the soundtrack, all the dialogue in the train sequence had to be re-recorded during postproduction.

- The walls in the compartments were mirrored, so great care had to be taken to make sure that the camera and mics didn't appear in the shots.

- Since all the scenes on the train were supposed to take place during a single trip, whenever the train reversed itself to travel back to London, the company had to move to the opposite side of the carriage to film so that the scenery outside the windows would always appear to be rushing past in the same direction.

By the time this initial portion of the shoot came to a close, most members of the crew had formed a favorable opinion of the Beatles, whom they found to be friendly, hardworking, and remarkably unaffected by the incredible attention that had recently come their way. The boys also got on well with their fellow cast members, especially Norman Rossington and John Junkin, with whom they remained friendly for years afterward. By most accounts, their relationship with Wilfrid Brambell, while respectful, was more distant, perhaps due to the significant difference in their ages.

Tuesday, March 10

Back on solid ground, the company moved to the Turk's Head Public House on Winchester Road in St. Margarets to film the scene in which Ringo visits a pub during his desertion from the group.

Wednesday, March 11

On its first day at Twickenham Film Studios, the company spent fourteen hours shooting the movie's first musical number—the Beatles serenading the schoolgirls with "I Should Have Known Better"—on a set built to resemble the train's luggage van.

Lester had not been happy with many of the screenplay's conceptions for the musical numbers, feeling that they were too contrived, so he tossed most of them out and devised his own. As written, the Beatles and the girls visit Grandfather, who has been imprisoned in the luggage van to keep him from causing any more trouble. Looking for something to do, John begins playing his mouth organ while the other Beatles accompany him using found objects to simulate the sounds of their instruments. Lester instead had the boys choose to play cards to alleviate their boredom. As the girls turn up to watch them, "I Should Have Known Better" starts playing on the soundtrack and then, in a surrealistic shift, the band members are suddenly shown holding their actual instruments, which they enthusiastically employ to perform the song. Once the song concludes, the instruments disappear and the scene shifts back to reality as the boys finish their card game.

To film the musical numbers, the prerecorded songs were played on the set during shooting as the band mimed their singing and performing to match the recordings. Lester found that because the Beatles had done so much lip-synching for their many television appearances, they were experts at this.

Thursday, March 12

The hotel room scenes, in which the Beatles shirk their assignment to answer fan mail and sneak out to a discotheque, then later discover a half-naked waiter in the closet (after Grandfather borrows the man's tux to go gambling at an exclusive club with an invitation purloined from Ringo), were filmed on a set at Twickenham.

Friday, March 13

The company traveled to Gatwick Airport South, twenty-seven miles south of London, to shoot the movie's closing sequence, in which the Beatles board their helicopter and fly away as Grandfather's forged-autographed photos rain down from the sky. The production couldn't afford to rent a helicopter, so Denis O'Dell called a friend who worked for British European Airways and worked out a product placement deal that permitted the filmmakers to use one of the airline's choppers free of charge as long as its corporate logo was prominently displayed. The airline's BEA logo was extended with TLES on the side of the helicopter to make it a suitable transport for the band.

After completing the departure scene, Gilbert Taylor and his camera crew went aloft in the BEA helicopter to film aerial shots of the Beatles cavorting on Gatwick's helicopter pad as part of the "escape" sequence, in which the boys break away from their claustrophobic existence by ducking out of the TV studio and running across a nearby vacant lot for a few minutes of uninhibited fun. Lester wanted the aerial shots to show the boys surrounded by open space, in contrast to the enclosed environments they'd been seen in up to that point.

Unfortunately, the camera's battery had not been properly charged, which caused the motor to slow down during filming. When motion picture film is shot at a speed slower than the standard twenty-four frames per second, the images speed up when projected at the regular rate. As a result, most of the Gatwick footage showed the Beatles cavorting in fast motion.

When he was first informed of this, Lester was upset, but, in an excellent example of his ability to make mistakes work for him, decided that when the ground-level portions of the scene were filmed a few weeks later, he would photograph them in fast motion as well. Likewise, because the production couldn't afford the proper camera stabilization equipment, many of the aerial images were extremely shaky, so Lester also vibrated the camera during the ground-level shoot. In the final sequence, the fast-paced, unstable footage gives the entire scene a wonderfully appropriate sense of urgency and excitement.

Monday, March 16

In the film, the Beatles' climactic concert is televised from a studio located within the facilities of the fictitious United

Television Company. The scene in which Grandfather persuades Ringo to desert the band was shot on a set constructed at Twickenham to represent the UTV canteen. Lester tossed an amusing sight gag into the piece by having an actor playing an actor costumed as a wounded soldier pour ketchup on his faux wound to freshen it up.

Tuesday, March 17

The film company moved to Les Ambassadeurs, an exclusive private club located in London's Hamilton Place, where scenes of Grandfather gambling in the club's casino, Le Cercle, were filmed.

Grandfather's busty companion in this sequence was Margaret Nolan, who was about to appear as James Bond's poolside masseuse, Dink, in *Goldfinger* (as well as the gold-covered girl in that film's main title sequence). The French croupier was played by Englishman Terry Hooper, a professional croupier who was then dating Prue Bury. When Bury learned that Lester was looking for someone to play the card dealer, she recommended her beau and he got the part.

When the Beatles, Norm, and Shake arrive at Le Cercle to corral Grandfather, Shake's line to the door guard—"I'm Ringo's sister"—was improvised by John Junkin.

Wednesday, March 18

The dressing room scene was filmed on a set at Twickenham
(in which a copy of *In His Own Write*, John's newly published
book of humorous poems and stories, was prominently displayed). In the bit where John cuts the tailor's tape measure
and says "I now declare this bridge open," the startled cloth-
ier is played by Dougie Millings, the band's real-life tailor.

Thursday, March 19–Friday, March 20

Thursday, March 19 was allegedly the day that the film found
its name.

The Beatles was never intended to be the movie's final
title—it was simply a placeholder until the creative team
could come up with something better. Walter Shenson had
thought they would name the film after one of the new songs;
however, once the tunes were finished, none of the titles
seemed appropriate. Other possibilities were considered,
including *Beatlemania*, *Traveling On*, *Moving On*, and *Let's
Go*, but none of them seemed ideal either. Riffing on the title
of the then-current West End hit *Oh What a Lovely War*,
John suggested *Oh What a Lovely Wart*.

The ultimate solution came from Ringo. Starr, who had
a propensity to garble the English language in oddly poetic
ways, had once described a grueling, all-night recording
session as "a hard day's night." John Lennon, a fan of clever

wordplay, was so taken with the phrase that he used it in a poem he wrote called "Sad Michael." John mentioned the expression to Walter Shenson on this Thursday, during a conversation in which Lennon told Shenson that Ringo sometimes said crazy things and the producer asked for an example. Shenson immediately sparked to the unusual phrase, as did Bud Ornstein, who was also in on the conversation. "We just got our title," Ornstein allegedly exclaimed. After running it past Lester and the Beatles, all of whom responded positively, Shenson submitted *A Hard Day's Night* to the United Artists executives in New York for approval.

At first the appellation was not well received, primarily because no one could understand what it meant. The UA execs bounced the phrase off of some young staff members and got a positive response, but they were still hesitant. Shenson said that he finally persuaded them to go with it by saying: "We're not going to improve on it. It's very provocative. It means nothing. It has nothing to do with the story. But it sounds like a Beatle title."

Thursday and Friday were spent at Twickenham filming scenes set in the corridors and staircases of the UTV complex, including several in which Grandfather interacts with the variety acts that are scheduled to appear on the television show along with the Beatles. One of these acts is a magician named Leslie Jackson, whose ten disappearing doves are reduced to nine after an unfortunate encounter with the senior McCartney. Jackson was portrayed by Derek Nimmo, who played a similar role for Lester in *It's Trad, Dad*.

The most notable corridor scene is John's solo moment, in which he encounters a young woman named Millie, who is sure she recognizes Lennon until he deftly persuades her that he couldn't possibly be who she thinks he is. This scene is arguably Alun Owen's finest piece of writing for the film: a wonderfully oblique pas de deux that whimsically underscores one of the most bittersweet aspects of the Beatles' fame—they were recognized by almost everyone and known by almost none. Millie was played by Anna Quayle, who had just returned to England after spending several years on Broadway starring in *Stop the World—I Want to Get Off*, for which she won a Tony Award for Best Performance by a Featured Actress in a Musical. John's wonderfully trenchant and melancholy final line—"She looks more like him than I do"—was not in the script: it was dubbed in during postproduction.

Monday, March 23–Thursday, March 26

The film's climactic concert scene required a fully equipped television studio. Since all the real studios in London were unavailable because they were in constant use, the filmmakers decided to build one of their own. The production rented a legitimate theater—the 1,132-seat Scala, located on Charlotte Street—and transformed it into a working studio by installing cameras and a sound system and constructing a control booth just off the main stage.

The production arranged to rent the necessary cameras and equipment from Bush Radio, a major British electronics company, for £20,000. Since this represented a hefty portion of the film's budget, Denis O'Dell decided to employ a little subterfuge to see if he could get a better deal. Bush's main rival was EMI, the parent company of the Beatles' record label, Parlophone. Confident that EMI would not want its superstar act associated with its biggest competitor, O'Dell called Sir Joseph Lockwood, the head of EMI, and fibbed that Bush had agreed to lend the movie all the television machinery it needed for free in exchange for the right to feature the Beatles in its ad campaigns. O'Dell told Lockwood that he was calling just to make sure that this was okay with him. As O'Dell had hoped, this was most certainly not okay with Sir Joseph, who immediately offered to provide the equipment free of charge.

The first scenes filmed in the Scala were those showing the Beatles rehearsing for their big show while tangling with a supercilious television director sporting an impossibly ugly mohair sweater, played by Welsh actor Victor Spinetti (future Tony Award winner for *Oh What a Lovely War*). The character was based on a real director whom Richard Lester, Alun Owen, and Spinetti knew well, so Lester's only direction to Spinetti was to "do" that fellow. During the shoot, Spinetti and the Beatles hit it off and became good friends (with the lads going so far as to join Spinetti's fan club).

Three musical numbers were featured in the rehearsal scenes. The first showed the band singing "If I Fell." As scripted, the number was supposed to start with a three-way drum duel among John, George, and Ringo. Lester dropped this and went straight into the song. George accidentally knocked over an amplifier during the performance. Lester decided to leave the goof in the film to enhance the scene's spontaneity.

The next number was Paul's ballad "And I Love Her." For this sequence, Lester wanted to show images of the band on the monitors in the control booth. To accomplish this, the film camera had to be run at twenty-five frames a second instead of twenty-four in order to eliminate the "shutter bar" that appears on television screens whenever they are photographed by a motion picture camera.

Lester also wanted to mount a second shot for the sequence in which the camera circled around Paul as he sang. To accomplish this, the camera was mounted on a child's swing hung from the Scala's ceiling. Operating the camera himself, Lester moved it slowly around McCartney as he performed. At one point, Lester aimed the lens directly into one of the movie lights, which produced a striking flare on the film. At the time, cinema aesthetics considered flares to be grievous technical errors that needed to be cut out, but Lester liked the way it looked and left it in. The effect soon became a rock 'n' roll movie staple.

In the screenplay, "I'm Happy Just to Dance with You" was preceded by an impromptu dance competition between the Beatles and a group of showgirls. On the day the scene was to be shot, Lester came up with the idea to do the number using stop-motion animation instead. The Beatles would be positioned on the stage alongside the showgirls, with all of them in frozen poses. Several frames of film would be exposed and then everyone would be moved into slightly different positions and photographed again. The idea was to eventually create a scene in which the Beatles zipped across the stage without ever moving their feet. The Lionel Blair Dancers were hired for the sequence (Blair was a popular actor, tap dancer, and choreographer who appeared regularly on British variety programs). However, after laboring for over three hours on the initial pose (allegedly prompting George to mutter, "I can't wait for take two"), Lester realized that executing his idea was going to take far more time than the film's tight schedule allowed, so he abandoned it.

All the musical numbers were shot with two or three cameras. The performances were filmed several times, with the multiple cameras repositioned each time in order to capture the number from every possible angle. The resulting footage was then edited together to create the final sequences.

Tuesday, March 31

Following a four-day Easter break, the company returned to the Scala to shoot the concert scene. The Beatles performed "Tell Me Why" and "She Loves You" for this scene, along with reprises of "I Should Have Known Better" and "If I Fell" and the B-side of their latest hit single, "You Can't Do That."

The concert required an audience, so 350 young students were hired from area drama schools, including future pop star Phil Collins, then a 13-year-old child actor. The students were engaged to play screaming fans, but since most of them were Beatles lovers in real life, not much acting was required.

Lester used seven cameras (all fitted with 10:1 zoom lenses) to shoot the sequence: three on the stage, three in the auditorium, and one in the control room. At the start of each number, Lester would tell the camera operators what aspects of the performance or the audience he wanted them to cover; then it was up to each individual operator to photograph everything of interest within his range. Unfortunately, one rather hopeless chap had a tendency to pan away anytime something intriguing was happening, so none of his footage was used. Lester moved back and forth among the cameras as filming progressed, making adjustments as necessary (he can be seen doing this in the film—crossing the stage during the "Tell Me Why" sequence). Ultimately, a remarkable 27,000 feet of film was exposed for the sequence, 17 minutes of which ended up in the final cut of the movie.

Between the loud music and the screaming audience, the noise level in the theater was extremely high. This was hard on the crew members—they couldn't hear each other or Lester, which made it hard for them to coordinate their actions. Cinematographer Gilbert Taylor was slightly deaf, so he was able to manage, but the decibel level was so high that it caused a new filling in camera operator Paul Wilson's mouth to vibrate with such intensity that it damaged the nerve in his tooth. The injury was so extensive that Wilson ultimately had to have the tooth removed.

Toward the end of the day, a large group of determined fans broke into the Scala by sawing the chains off an upper-level fire door and swarming down into the top tiers of the auditorium, where they tried to mix in with the drama students. Lester reported having to protect himself and the Beatles with a tripod when they encountered some of the overzealous invaders in a stairwell.

Wednesday, April 1–Thursday, April 2

Following the concert scene, the company spent two more days at the Scala. They were scheduled to film several scenes that took place outside the theater: the Beatles' arrival in their chauffeured car; portions of John, Paul, and George's search for Ringo; and Grandfather's attempts to hawk his forged-autographed pictures of the boys to fans waiting to see the show. Things went smoothly at first, but on Thursday morning a large crowd gathered and threatened to get out of hand, so the police told Lester that he had to stop working and get off the street.

Needing something to shoot so the day wouldn't go to waste, the director decided to film a scene that was originally supposed to be done toward the end of the schedule: a press reception at which the Beatles turn the tables on a group of patronizing reporters by giving nonsense answers to their ridiculous questions. Alun Owen based this sequence on a reception that the Beatles had attended at the British embassy in Washington, D.C. The boys had been treated with appalling condescension by the assembled diplomats and finally walked out after one of the dignitaries snipped off a lock of Ringo's hair without permission. As originally scripted, the reception was supposed to take place in a hotel ballroom, but Lester decided to use the Scala's dress circle lounge instead.

To play the fictitious members of the fourth estate, Lester pulled some real reporters and photographers in off the street (one of the photographers had a motor-driven camera, which inspired the director to improvise the amusing bit in which George makes a series of silly faces into the camera, the photos of which then pop up onscreen in rapid succession). Lester also called some actor friends who lived nearby and asked them to come in.

The director wrote down a series of questions (some of which were in the screenplay and many of which were not) for the reporters to ask. The Beatles responded with a combination of scripted answers and improvised ones. (When the sequence was edited, Lester mismatched some of the questions and answers for comedic effect.) It's not clear who came up with the reception's most famous retort—Ringo's responding to a question asking if he is a mod or a rocker by saying, "I'm a mocker." Walter Shenson insisted that Alun Owen wrote the line, although it does not appear in the shooting script. It's possible that Owen did craft the bit after the script was finished, although authorship has also been attributed to Lester and to Ringo himself. Whoever wrote it, the line is inarguably one of the scene's highlights.

Sunday, April 5 / Sunday, April 12

On two consecutive weekends, the company assembled at London's Marylebone Station to shoot the movie's opening sequence, in which a crowd of screaming fans chase the Beatles though the streets, into the station, and onto the train. Marylebone was chosen because it was the only terminal in London that ever closed. As it did so only on Sundays, the cast and crew had to give up their day of rest, but in exchange they got the full run of the place.

The opening shot of the film—John, George, and Ringo racing toward the camera with a group of zealous admirers in hot pursuit—was photographed on Boston Place, a narrow street adjacent to the station. As the boys ran, George fell down and Ringo tripped over him, causing John to dissolve into laughter. Once again enjoying the spontaneity, Lester decided to leave the spill in the movie.

Despite the creative team's agreement to show the Beatles performing only in real-life situations, Alun Owen had scripted a big opening number for the film: upon entering the station, Lennon, Harrison, and Starr were to run to the platform where their train was waiting, grab their instruments off a luggage pile, and launch into a song. Like a rifle shot fired overhead, the first note of the tune was to stop the mob dead in its tracks as Paul arrived with his grandfather and joined his bandmates to finish the performance.

The Beatles objected to this sequence, feeling it was corny. Lester agreed and instead shot a number of vignettes showing John, George, and Ringo attempting to shake the crowd by jumping over barriers and hiding in coffee shops, phone booths, and photo kiosks while a disguised Paul and his grandfather make their way to the train. These scenes were intercut with a sequence in which Norm—anxiously awaiting the lads' arrival—obtains a bag of milk from a vending machine and struggles to open it, only to end up with a mouthful of plastic (this was another of Lester's on-the-spot improvs: while scouting the station, the director spied the vending machine, thought the idea of milk in a bag was amusing, and worked it into the scene).

At the end of one of the Sundays, the Beatles climbed into their chauffeured car to be driven home. Lester put a camera in the car with them and photographed the group reacting to a crowd of real fans that swarmed the vehicle as it left Marylebone. Lester later incorporated this footage into the scene where the Beatles are driven away from the train station after arriving in London. Since the boys had already changed out of their costumes, the outfits they are wearing do not match those they wear in the rest of the train sequence.

Monday, April 6–Wednesday, April 8

The next three days were spent filming on sets at Twickenham. The scene set in the UTV makeup room, during which Grandfather expresses the core concept of the movie by complaining that all he's done during his time with the

Beatles is "been in a train and a room, a car and a room, and a room and a room," was begun on Monday and finished on Tuesday morning.

Tuesday afternoon was devoted to shooting the scenes that took place inside the police station. Liverpool native Deryck Guyler, who narrated Lester's *It's Trad, Dad*, played the station's gruff-but-hospitable sergeant.

Wednesday was spent filming Grandfather's attempts to hide in the studio basement and his accidental triggering of the stage elevator, which causes him to rise up into the middle of a rehearsal of a Strauss operetta. As the Beatles were not needed for this scene, they were given the day off.

Not working on the movie didn't mean that the boys weren't working. In fact, the Beatles found the pace of the shoot to be relatively leisurely when compared to the grueling schedule they had been keeping for the past eighteen months. "We didn't know how long it took to make a movie," Paul McCartney recalled. "[In the same amount of time] we could have done a couple of tours, written a few new songs, and cut an album." So they pursued a full roster of outside activities during production: they appeared on several radio and television programs; attended the Variety Clubs of Great Britain luncheon on March 19 and the Carl Alan dance awards on March 23; and taped segments for a variety show called *Around the Beatles* that was scheduled to air on Associated Rediffusion TV on April 28.

Thursday, April 9

The scene in which Ringo, playing hooky from the band, meets a young boy named Charlie, who is playing hooky from school, was filmed on a towpath located alongside the River Thames in Kew. The script called for an eight-year-old boy and one was cast, but he had difficulty with his lines and was replaced by fourteen-year-old David Jaxon (playing ten), who had been hired as a backup in case the younger child wasn't able to handle the part.

The scene begins with several shots of Ringo wandering aimlessly, which were filmed because Starr had arrived on set feeling hungover and needed some time to warm up before tackling a dialogue scene. Ringo and Charlie meet when the lad accidentally rolls a tire into the errant drummer. Various members of the crew—Lester included—attempted to hit Starr with the tire but couldn't manage it. Finally, Lester had Jaxon take a turn, and he bowled the Beatle over on the first try.

Friday, April 10

George's encounter with a sexy UTV secretary (played by Alison Seebohm) was filmed this day on a set at Twickenham.

Monday, April 13

Continuing at Twickenham, the morning was spent shooting George's solo scene, in which Harrison is mistaken for a "typical" teenager by Simon Marshall, a neurotic, trend-obsessed television executive in charge of UTV's youth programming. In the course of the scene, Marshall becomes increasingly flustered by the Beatle's skewering of the phony teen idol the executive has conjured up to persuade young people to buy his sponsor's products. This was one of Alun Owen's best scenes: a brilliant satire of both marketing and the generation gap. Marshall was played by the respected stage actor Kenneth Haigh, who had starred in the original West End and Broadway productions of John Osborne's landmark play *Look Back in Anger* and was currently appearing in *Caligula* at London's Phoenix Theater. A friend of Alun Owen, Haigh appeared in *A Hard Day's Night* without credit, allegedly because he felt that appearing in a pop musical would be detrimental to his reputation as a serious actor.

Owen introduced a colorful bit of Liverpool slang into the scene's dialogue: "grotty" (short for grotesque). The dialogue suggests that this is a word George used frequently. In fact, neither he nor the other Beatles had ever heard the term before, although they did adopt it afterward. (John Lennon felt that Alun Owen sometimes played up his northern identity to the point of caricature and once accused the playwright of being "a professional Liverpudlian," to which Owen famously replied, "Well, I supposed that's better than being an amateur Liverpudlian.")

The afternoon was spent filming the scene in which George teaches Shake to shave in the bathroom of their hotel suite by spraying foam on the mirror and then scraping Shake's reflection. This scene was not in the original screenplay but was added after Alun Owen, Richard Lester, and Walter Shenson saw how well Harrison was coming across onscreen and decided to give him more to do.

John also appears in the scene, playing with a toy submarine in the bubble-filled tub. In the segment's surreal ending, Lennon sinks out of sight beneath the bubbles (Shenson wanted this bit redone because John's swimsuit is briefly visible as he submerges, but Lester liked Lennon's performance and opted to keep it). Eager to hurry John along to the TV studio, Norm empties the tub, only to find that Lennon has disappeared. As Norm frets over the Beatle's fate (did he somehow go down the drain?), John suddenly appears behind the frazzled manager. As written, the bit was meant to end with Lennon pondering the tub along with Norm and saying, "I wonder how I did that?" but Lester ultimately decided to finish by having John simply hurry Norm out of the room without ever addressing the matter.

Tuesday, April 14

A fake traffic jam was created on Arlington Road in St. Margarets for a scene in which the Beatles' car gets stuck behind a bus on the way to the TV studio.

At some point during this day, Walter Shenson asked John and Paul to write a song called "A Hard Day's Night" to go along with the film's new title—a fast-paced, up-tempo number along the lines of "Twist and Shout." Since there was no place in the film where the boys could perform the tune, the plan was to run it under the opening titles. Lennon and McCartney were reportedly not thrilled with the prospect of having to pen yet another song for the film, but John finally agreed to take on the task and wrote the piece that night on the back of a birthday card that he had bought for his son, Julian. Lennon and McCartney performed the song the next morning for Shenson and Lester, who loved it.

Wednesday, April 15

The company returned to the Scala Theater to finish the outdoor scenes that had been aborted on April 2. The unit began shooting very early in the morning so that filming could wrap before school let out and the young fans started turning up again.

Thursday, April 16

The exterior of St. John's Secondary School at 83 Clarendon Road in Notting Hill Gate doubled as a police station for the exterior shots of the bobbies pursuing the Beatles (and the Beatles pursuing the bobbies) in and out of the cop house during the movie's big chase sequence. Once these shots were completed, the balance of the day was spent filming the police officers (all played by professional extras) chasing the Beatles up and down the neighboring streets.

That night, the Beatles went to Abbey Road Studios to record the movie's new title song. Journalist and friend of the band Maureen Cleave rode with John to the session and inspired a key change in the lyrics. When Cleave commented that she thought the lines "When I get home to you / I find my tiredness is through / And I feel alright" were "rather . . . feeble," Lennon borrowed her pen and immediately changed them to "When I get home to you / I find the things that you do / Will make me feel all right."

Richard Lester was present at the session and requested that the song have a "blockbuster" beginning since it was going to open the film. This led George Martin to suggest that the song start with a single, powerful chord that would grab people's attention. The striking and unique sound that the band came up with was the result of George, Paul, and John simultaneously playing a combination of notes on their respective instruments (Harrison's a newly acquired twelve-string Rickenbacker; McCartney's electric bass; Lennon's six-string acoustic guitar), with enhancements by Ringo on snare drum and ride cymbal and George Martin on piano.

The basic song was recorded in nine takes, and then some additional portions— including George's riveting guitar solo—were overdubbed. The song's jangling fade-out was prompted by Richard Lester's request to end the song with something "dreamy" that would create a segue from the film's opening credits into the movie proper. The "swirling" sound of the fade was accomplished by dubbing George's guitar work onto the master tape at half-speed.

Friday, April 17

The title of the film was officially announced to the press on this day. Meanwhile, the unit returned to Les Ambassadeurs to film the discotheque scene in the Garrison Room, a popular night spot located in the club's basement. During the scene, Ringo dances with a very tall man who teaches him to dance in an extremely eccentric manner that includes lots of jumping up and down. The tall man was played by writer/actor Jeremy Lloyd (future cast member of *Rowan*

& Martin's Laugh-In and co-creator of the long-running sitcom *Are You Being Served?*). Lloyd was not attempting to be comedic in the scene—that was actually the way the man danced.

Saturday, April 18

The Beatles spent the morning at Twickenham, re-recording their dialogue for the train scene. Lester found that they were as good at dubbing as they were at lip-synching.

Monday, April 20–Tuesday, April 21

Two days were spent at the Jack Billings TV School of Dancing on Goldhawk Road in Shepherd's Bush, photographing a scene in which Paul, searching the UTV complex for Ringo after the drummer has gone missing, stumbles into a rehearsal studio, where he finds a young actress—played by nineteen-year-old Isla Blair—dressed in Restoration period costume and rehearsing her dialogue for an upcoming show in a stiff, "actressy" manner. Paul teases the girl and offers her some down-to-earth Liverpudlian advice designed to help her sound more authentic. Offended, the actress rejects Paul's suggestions. McCartney departs, but on his way out, he overhears the young woman adjusting her performance in accordance with his tips. She sounds terrific and he is delighted.

The scene was a troublesome one. It was very long (one take ran almost eight minutes) and some of the dialogue was awkward and needed to be rewritten on the set. The piece also contained some complicated choreography—Lester wanted the camera to spin around McCartney and Blair during the scene, requiring the two performers to carefully coordinate their movements with those of the Arriflex. Finally, Paul was very self-conscious and came across rather stiffly, necessitating numerous retakes. Unlike the other Beatles, Paul had a strong interest in "serious" culture, especially the theater, and Lester later commented that he felt Paul's desire to be a good actor sometimes led him to try too hard. As for the other Beatles, Lester felt that Ringo was the most natural actor of the group; John had the most electrifying personality; and George was the most accurate performer ("He never attempted to do too much or too little but everything he did was spot on").

Wednesday, April 22

The company spent this day in the streets, filming several outdoor scenes in various locations around London. To keep the crowds at bay, diversionary measures were taken. Denis O'Dell would send a few crew members and some extras to a spot several blocks away from where the unit was actually planning to shoot; the decoy group would mill about as if they were preparing to film and the fans would gravitate there, thinking the Beatles would soon arrive; meanwhile, the main unit would grab the scenes they needed in the real location. The diversions usually didn't last long: the fans would eventually discover the ruse and head for the true filming site. As a result, most of these scenes were done in one or two takes, because as soon as the crowd gathered, the company would have to move on.

The day began with the boys running down a fire escape outside the Odeon Cinema in Hammersmith, the start of the "escape" scene. Then the company returned to Notting Hill Gate to film an unscripted gag for the chase scene in which a thief—played by Lester's friend, actor John Bluthal—attempts to break into a car just as the police come running by in pursuit of the Beatles. After several foiled attempts, the thief finally manages to gain entry to the vehicle, only to have a cop jump in alongside him and commandeer the car for use in the chase.

Several vignettes for Ringo's "desertion" sequence were filmed on Lancaster and All Saints roads: Starr photographing a milk bottle, being chased by fans, and ducking into a secondhand shop to buy a disguise. Finally, Paul was filmed entering the Jack Billings TV School of Dancing (which had a new sign hung over the door identifying it as a "TV Rehearsal Room")—the opening shot for his scene with Isla Blair.

Thursday, April 23

The company spent the day filming ground-level shots for the "escape" sequence at the Thornbury Playing Fields in Isleworth. A fake helicopter landing pad was constructed on the site so that it would resemble the original Gatwick Airport location. To match the footage filmed at Gatwick, shots of the boys playing in the field were photographed in fast motion using a shaky handheld camera. To provide some contrast, Lester decided to film some slow-motion shots of the Beatles falling through space, which were created by having the boys jump off ladders.

John left early that day to attend a literary luncheon celebrating the publication of *In His Own Write*, so he didn't participate in the afternoon's filming. To cover his absence, Lester photographed several shots of the boys dancing on the landing pad using a subjective camera to simulate John's first-person point of view. Donning Lennon's trousers and shoes, Lester operated the camera for these shots himself. As a result, the feet glimpsed briefly in those clips, meant to be John's, are actually Lester's.

In the screenplay, Lennon delivered the scene's final line—"Gee mister, we're sorry we hurt your field"—to the lot's owner, who has just kicked them off. Since John wasn't there, the line was given to George instead.

Friday, April 24

The final morning of production was spent in West Ealing, shooting the vignette from Ringo's desertion sequence in which the gallant drummer lays down his coat to allow a beautiful young woman to step across a series of puddles, only to inadvertently place the coat over a workman's hole, into which the lady then tumbles. When the scene was finished, filming on *A Hard Day's Night* was complete.

That afternoon, a wrap party was held in a private hall behind the Turk's Head Pub. There was a lot to celebrate. Despite the intensity of the shoot, it had been a positive experience for just about every member of the cast and crew (John Junkin referred to the production as the six happiest working weeks of his life), all of whom had done exemplary work under some very difficult conditions. Much of the credit for this went to Richard Lester, whose creative energy, collaborative nature, and ability to remain unfailingly polite, good-humored, and calm in the midst of often chaotic circumstances proved to be an inspiration to everyone involved. The Beatles led the unit in celebrating their director by pouring red wine over Lester's head and giving him a card that read: "To Walt Disney: Thanks for directing us, sir. From your favorite actors: John, Paul, Ringo, and Gary."

As the party wound down, everyone began to go their separate ways. Ringo had nothing to do that night, so he went home with Lester and had dinner with the director and his family.

CHAPTER 6

It Won't Be Long

With filming complete, there were only about six weeks left to finish the movie. Knowing that they wouldn't have much time, Richard Lester and John Jympson had actually begun editing the picture while it was still shooting, so they had a rough cut ready just a few days after the production wrapped. They now had to refine it.

Lester took the same loose, improvisational approach to editing as he had to shooting—he didn't worry about creating a neat match between shots and never hesitated to radically reshape a scene or a sequence if he thought it would make the movie better. In keeping with Lester's desire to have *A Hard Day's Night* reflect the Beatles' terrific energy and zest, he and Jympson cut the film to move at a very rapid pace. The only exceptions were the musical numbers, which were slowed down so that viewers could give their full attention to the songs (the performance scenes were cut to the beat of the music, with two-bar edits, four-bars edits, and so on).

As the film took shape, a number of elements were changed. Many scenes were trimmed and tightened:

- The scene where Paul prevents his grandfather from becoming engaged to the rich lady on the train originally continued to show Paul getting into a tug-of-war with the woman over Grandfather as the Beatles are besieged by everyone they've met during the trip, including the businessman and the schoolgirls. All of the latter material was removed and Grandfather's "Congratulate me boys, I'm engaged!" bit was reshot on a set at Twickenham to provide a smoother transition into the luggage van sequence.

- Lester was unhappy with most of Grandfather's scenes—he ultimately came to feel that the character was too much of a contrivance and that Wilfrid Brambell had too often overplayed his performance—so a running gag in which Grandfather continually interferes with a juggling act was completely removed from the TV studio sequence and the rest of the old mixer's scenes were scaled back whenever possible.

- The concert scene was also scaled back: "You Can't Do That" was dropped and "I Should Have Known Better" and "If I Fell" were shortened. As the concert scene was assembled, Lester and Jympson were so taken with footage of one female audience member's dramatically tearful reaction to the band that they cut back to her again and again during "She Loves You." They didn't know the identity of the girl—who was wearing a sailor-style blouse—so they nicknamed her "White Rabbit."

The scene order was sometimes switched around. The most significant change involved George's encounter with Simon Marshall. In the screenplay, the scene took place in the middle of the band's hunt for the AWOL Ringo: while searching the UTV complex for his friend, George was to accidentally stumble into Marshall's office. During production, the scene was moved up to the "break" sequence, in which the Beatles take a breather after rehearsing "I'm Happy Just to Dance with You." Since the scene was now going to come just before the canteen scene in which Grandfather urges Ringo to desert the band, a new introduction was shot that showed Harrison heading for the canteen—he would now wander into Marshall's office on his way to meet Starr. A tag was also filmed that had George finally arrive at the canteen after leaving Marshall's office just as Ringo storms out to go "parading." Harrison tries to tell Starr what just happened to him, but the irritated drummer stalks off before he can. During the final edit, it was decided to move the Marshall scene up even farther, to just after John's encounter with Millie. The introduction was moved along with it, but the tag remained where it was. As a result, with almost twenty minutes of screen time separating the Marshall scene and the tag, Harrison's "Do you know what happened to me?" line to Ringo appears to come out of nowhere in the finished film.

Two scenes were dropped entirely: the one in which the boys get caught in a traffic jam on the way to the studio and Paul's solo encounter with Isla Blair, which was removed because its great length slowed the film's pacing considerably and because of Paul's awkward performance.

The mood during editing was tense—in part because Lester and Jympson were working practically around the clock to get the picture done on time and also because Walter Shenson had become very anxious. Concerned that they had rushed through production too quickly on too low a budget, the producer began to worry that the end result wasn't going to be very good. His pessimistic attitude spread to other members of the team, who now feared that their labor of love might be a turkey.

By the end of the first week in May, the fine cut of the movie—running a brisk eighty-seven minutes—was complete. Lester and Shenson showed it to David Picker, Bud

Ornstein, and Arnold Picker on May 7. Arnold Picker brought his wife to the screening. To Lester's horror, Mrs. Picker began making what sounded to him like a disapproving "tch tch" sound every time something of note happened on screen. From the constancy of the lady's reactions, it appeared to Lester that she hated every aspect of the movie, and by the time the screening was over, the director—whose confidence had already been badly shaken by Shenson's pessimism—was convinced that his film was a complete and utter failure. He was therefore quite surprised (and greatly relieved) when Mrs. Picker began praising the movie extravagantly. As it turned out, "tch tch" was her unique way of showing approval, not disapproval.

David Picker, Arnold Picker, and Bud Ornstein were surprised by the movie—they weren't expecting something so offbeat and unconventional—but they recognized that it was new, fresh, and exciting. They loved it and were convinced it was going to be a big hit. The executives' only concern was that the Beatles' Liverpudlian accents might be too thick for American audiences to understand. One of them suggested that the boys' voices be dubbed by American actors for the U.S. release, a notion that Lester and Shenson immediately rejected. Even if they hadn't, it probably would have been impossible to get the Beatles to go along: when Paul heard about the suggestion, he responded, "If we can understand a cowboy talkin' Texan, they can understand us talkin' Liverpool."

With the picture locked, it was now time to add some finishing touches. Sound editor Gordon Daniel got to work layering in the necessary background sounds and effects, while Robert Freeman created a distinctive credit sequence for the end of the film. The screenplay had suggested that the end credits play over a shot of one of the many pictures of the Beatles that rain down from the helicopter in the movie's final shot. Wanting something more interesting, Lester and Shenson called upon Freeman, the photographer and designer who created the iconic black-and-white album cover for *With the Beatles* and was the production's on-set photographer (along with the band's old friend Astrid Kirchherr). Freeman shot a series of black-and-white photos of each Beatle, which he then dissolved in and out of one another as the names of the cast and crew rolled by. Backed by a reprise of "A Hard Day's Night," the sequence was elegant, witty, and effective.

Freeman also created a poster for the film's UK release. United Artists had produced a poster for American theaters that featured one photo of each Beatle, cut off below the eyes to emphasize their "mop top" haircuts and placed on a white background surrounded by cartoon drawings of girls jumping up and down alongside a cartoon guitar. Neither Shenson nor Lester liked it, so they asked Freeman to come up with something different. Feeling that a single photo couldn't capture the energy and animation that the Beatles showed onscreen, Freeman decided to use multiple pictures of each Beatle (taken from the photos used for the end credit montage), arranged in rows to resemble strips of motion-picture film against a blue background. A single picture of Wilfrid Brambell was dropped into the middle of the array (on Paul's row).

Although the movie was filled with Beatles songs, musical scores were required for several of the nonperformance scenes. For these, Lester opted to do something unusual. Up until that point, film scores had always been instrumental. Songs were not used unless they were performed onscreen or were part of a title sequence. Lester changed all that when he decided to use songs—Beatles songs, of course—to score the nonsinging scenes, thus initiating a practice that was continued in influential films such as *The Graduate* and *American Graffiti* and is now an industry standard.

- To score the nightclub scene, Lester used three tunes from the band's *With the Beatles*: "I Wanna Be Your Man" (written by Paul and John and originally recorded by the Rolling Stones before being redone by the Beatles with

Ringo singing the lead); "Don't Bother Me" (written and sung by George); and "All My Loving" (a McCartney-penned tune that Lester loved).

- To score the madcap chase between the Beatles and the police at the end of the film, Lester chose the band's current number one single: "Can't Buy Me Love." Written by Paul in January 1964 while the Beatles were in France, the song was recorded on January 29, 1964 at EMI's Pathe Marconi Studios in Paris. Additional guitar and vocal overdubs were taped at Abbey Road on February 25, the same day the group began recording the movie songs. Lester liked the tune's energy and was eager to include it in the film.

- A song was also required for the "escape" scene. The screenplay had the boys running around the field playing a pantomime game of soccer with an imaginary ball. During filming, Lester dropped this notion and instead shot a lot of footage of the lads larking about, which he then chopped up and intercut. By the time the scene was finished, it had become more of a montage than a straightforward narrative, and Lester wanted a fast-paced song to give it cohesion. None of the available tunes seemed appropriate, so Lester asked John to come up with a new piece. John went to work and quickly wrote "I'll Cry Instead," which was recorded at Abbey Road on

June 1. However, when Lester heard the finished product, he felt that the song's downbeat lyrics weren't appropriate for the high-spirited "escape," so he decided to reuse "Can't Buy Me Love" instead.

- Instrumental music was required for two scenes in the film: Ringo's desertion and the sequence in which Grandfather runs back to the theater after escaping from the police station. Since the pattern of using Beatles songs had already been established, it was decided to use instrumental versions of the band's compositions rather than original material. Lester chose "This Boy" for Ringo's walkabout because it had an appropriately melancholy air. For Grandfather's part, he chose a jazzed-up version of "A Hard Day's Night."

- George Martin arranged the pieces and assembled a group of session musicians to record them, including guitarist Vic Flick, whose distinctive plucking had energized John Barry's classic arrangement of "The James Bond Theme." Flick added a similar texture to the instrumental version of "This Boy," which was renamed "Ringo's Theme" for the film.

Martin recorded the instrumentals on June 8. Lester was present for the session and at some point criticized one of Martin's arrangements. Martin took exception to Lester's comments, and the exchange quickly became heated. Martin eventually revised the music to Lester's specifications, but after that the two men rarely spoke.

The film's final sound mix was done at Twickenham Studios under the supervision of Recording Director Stephen Dalby. When it came time to mix the concert scene, Lester wanted the sound levels turned up as high as possible in order to approximate the volume of an actual concert. Worried that this would create distortion on the movie's optical soundtrack, the technicians were hesitant to do it, but Lester insisted, feeling that if any distortion did occur, it would only help make the scene sound more like the real thing.

By the middle of June, the film's negative had been cut and the individual elements sent to the lab so that it could begin making all the prints necessary for *A Hard Day's Night*'s worldwide release.

As the film was being finished, the soundtrack album was also being prepared. This had required some intensive negotiations: when EMI first learned about the Beatles' soundtrack deal with United Artists, the corporation's officials were understandably upset. Although soundtrack albums were indeed not mentioned in Parlophone's contract with the band, EMI did not agree with Noel Rodgers that this meant that the Beatles were free to produce one for another record company. EMI felt that its contract with the

Fab Four implicitly covered all forms of recorded music, mentioned and unmentioned. The company's position was reasonably solid and, had the matter gone to court, there is a good chance that EMI could have prevailed.

However, at the time the Beatles made their deal with UA, Capitol had not yet agreed to release the band's work in the United States, and EMI probably realized that the arrangement could provide a way to finally get the Beatles' music into the American market. So a new deal was worked out that permitted United Artists Records to release the songs created for *A Hard Day's Night* on a soundtrack album in the United States, while EMI would release them in the UK (through Parlophone) and in the rest of the world (through its other subsidiaries and licensees). After the Beatles' popularity exploded and Capitol began releasing their music in the States, the deal was further amended to allow the EMI subsidiary to also put out the songs in America on an album of its own, as long as that album did not specifically reference the movie. Capitol was also given the exclusive right to issue the film's songs as singles in the United States.

As a result of this agreement, two different versions of the soundtrack album were created: one for EMI and the other for UAR.

- The Parlophone iteration contained all the songs created for the film: "A Hard Day's Night," "I Should Have Known

Better," "If I Fell," "Tell Me Why," "And I Love Her," "I'm Happy Just to Dance with You," and "I'll Cry Instead" (the album lineup was finalized before the song was dropped from the movie). "Can't Buy Me Love" and "You Can't Do That" were also included. It was Parlophone's practice to re-release its Beatles singles in EP collections. Because "Can't" was featured so prominently in *A Hard Day's Night*, Parlophone decided to re-release it and its B-side on the movie album instead.

More songs were needed to produce a full-length album (the band's previous Parlophone LPs had each contained fourteen tracks). The three tunes from the nightclub scene could not be used because they were already on *With the Beatles*, so on June 1, after the band finished "I'll Cry Instead," they began recording an additional batch of songs to fill out the LP. Most of these had been written during a three-week vacation the boys took in May. They included three written by John—"I'll Be Back," "Any Time at All," and "When I Get Home"— and one by Paul—"Things We Said Today."

The album was issued in both mono and stereo. The versions of some of the songs on the stereo edition featured takes, edits, or mixes different from those on the mono edition. The mono version was also released on reel-to-reel tape. The album cover featured an adaptation of Robert Freeman's photo-strip poster design (minus Wilfrid Brambell).

- The United Artists version of the soundtrack contained the seven film songs, as well as "Can't Buy Me Love," which EMI gave UAR permission to include because of its significant role in the picture. However, EMI would not allow United Artists to use "You Can't Do That" or any of the other tunes created to augment the Parlophone LP. Since UAR only had the right to utilize the film songs, the album was filled out with George Martin's instrumental versions of "A Hard Day's Night" and "This Boy," along with instrumental versions of "I Should Have Known Better" and "And I Love Her."

   UAR's version of the soundtrack was also released in both mono and stereo. It sported a red cover featuring the half photos of each Beatle from the American movie poster.

Two additional albums were also prepared:

- To further capitalize on the only Beatles songs to which it had the rights, United Artists commissioned George Martin to create instrumental versions of all the film's tunes, which were assembled (along with instrumental versions of other Beatles songs) in a collection officially titled *A Hard Day's Night: Instrumental Versions of the*

Motion Picture Score, but informally known as *By Popular Demand*, after the words that appear on a banner stamped on the record's cover. A number of instrumental singles were also released, including one of the title track.

- Capitol Records put out an eleven-song variation on the Parlophone album. *Something New* featured "I'll Cry Instead," "Things We Said Today," "Any Time at All," "When I Get Home," "Tell Me Why," "And I Love Her," "I'm Happy Just to Dance with You," and "If I Fell." "A Hard Day's Night" was not included because Capitol was not allowed to tie its record to the movie. "I Should Have Known Better," "Can't Buy Me Love," "You Can't Do That," and "I'll Be Back" were also omitted and replaced by two songs from the *Long Tall Sally* EP—"Slow Down" and "Matchbox"—and "Komm, Gib Mir Deine Hand," a German-language recording of "I Wanna Hold Your Hand" that had been produced for the German market. Parlophone also released an edition of *Something New* for sale only on American armed forces bases in Europe. EMI released it in Germany on the Odeon label.

Advance orders on both the Parlophone and UAR versions of the soundtrack were record-setting—250,000 in the UK; 1,000,000 in the United States—and, as Bud Ornstein had predicted, more than covered the cost of the movie.

Thanks to these albums, the film was already in profit a month before it was released.

CHAPTER 7

We Hope You Will Enjoy the Show

The music came first.

United Artists Records released its version of the *A Hard Day's Night* soundtrack in the United States on June 26, 1964. It went straight to the top of the album charts, where it stayed for 14 weeks, and sold 2 million copies in three months, making it one of the fastest-selling LPs in history. Parlophone issued its iteration in the UK on July 10. It entered the charts at number one and eventually sold over 800,000 copies.

Most critics and fans agree that the Parlophone version of *A Hard Day's Night* is the album in which the Beatles came into their own musically. It was the first of the band's LPs to consist entirely of original material (their previous collections both contained a generous helping of covers). It was—and remains—the only Beatles album on which every song was written by John Lennon and/or Paul McCartney, who in a few short years had progressed from writing competent, if routine love songs to crafting innovative works of astonishing musical and lyrical sophistication. (It was following *A Hard Day's Night* that critics began seriously comparing the duo to the likes of George and Ira Gershwin, Cole Porter, and even Wolfgang Amadeus Mozart.) It was the record on which—with the addition of George's jangling twelve-string Rickenbacker guitar and four-track recording to the group's instrumental arsenal—the Beatles' rich, dense, and buoyant sound came into full flower, generating a string of classic songs (including the title track) and setting the stage for the three masterworks (*Rubber Soul*, *Revolver*, and *Sgt. Pepper's Lonely Hearts Club Band*) that followed. At the time of its release, *A Hard Day's Night* was judged to be the band's best album to date; it is still considered one of their finest.

Parlophone issued "A Hard Day's Night" as a single (b/w "Things We Said Today") in the UK on July 10. Three days later, Capitol released its edition of the single (b/w "I Should Have Known Better") in the United States. Both quickly went to number one and by the first week of August, both albums and both singles were in the number one position on their respective charts in their respective countries, the first and only time such a thing has ever happened.

Capitol released *Something New* on July 20, and the album spent nine weeks on the U.S. charts in second place, right behind UAR's *A Hard Day's Night*. The combined sales of all three versions of the album came to well over four million copies, making it the biggest-selling soundtrack ever to that point. *A Hard Day's Night: Instrumental Versions of the Motion Picture Score* came out later in the year, but because it did not actually feature the Beatles, it did not do as well as the other records.

Thousands of fans filled Piccadilly Circus on Monday, July 6, 1964, to greet the Beatles as they arrived at the London Pavilion for the royal premiere of *A Hard Day's Night*. Because the Queen had recently given birth and was convalescing, Princess Margaret attended in her stead.

There were a few snafus: the Pavilion's organist had not finished his preshow serenade when the film started, so the projectionist muted the first few seconds of the movie's soundtrack to allow the performer to finish and thus completely ruined the impact of the title song's powerful opening chord. And despite Lester's efforts to ensure that the final concert was mixed as loudly as possible, the projectionist turned the volume down during that scene so as not to disturb the Princess. Despite these problems, the invitation-only audience loved the movie and applauded enthusiastically at the end.

The Beatles had actually seen the film for the first time the previous Saturday. Nervous about the boys' reaction, Richard Lester hadn't attended that screening. Walter Shenson did and reported that after the movie was over, none of the Beatles said a word until George finally stood up and announced: "Well, I liked it. I think it's very good," at which point the others expressed their enthusiasm as well. Even John—who in later years would sometimes criticize the film for its "comic book" portrayal of the Beatles as "cheeky, but lovable mop tops"—enjoyed the picture, telling a reporter that he thought it was better than all the other pop musicals, although "not as good as James Bond."

A second premiere was held in Liverpool on July 10, after which the movie opened in 160 theaters throughout the United Kingdom. On August 12—following several weeks of intensive promotion and advance screenings sponsored by local radio stations—*A Hard Day's Night* opened in over 700 theaters and drive-ins across the United States. Beatles fans in both countries turned out in droves to see the film, often screaming as loudly when their idols appeared on the screen as their concertgoing counterparts did when the boys appeared onstage. The movie continued to open in territories around the world through September. With over 1,500 prints playing around the globe, Arnold Picker bragged that there were more copies of *A Hard Day's Night* in circulation than there had been of any other film in history.

Apart from a few critics who could not get past their dislike of pop music, the film's unusual visual technique, or the lads' thick scouses, most viewers gave the film excellent reviews:

- "Instead of the raw excuse for Beatle-song which I expected, here was a sharply professional piece, directed with great dash by Richard Lester, boldly photographed by Gilbert Taylor, and smartly edited by John Jympson—and acted . . . with the most likable aplomb by the Sacred Four." —Dilys Powell, *Sunday Times*

- "*A Hard Day's Night* is a whacky, offbeat piece of filming, charged with vitality and inventiveness by director Dick Lester, slickly lensed and put over at a fair lick." —Rich, *Variety*

- "Walter Shenson's 85-minute production . . . [has] all the ingredients of good cinema—wonderful photography, imaginative direction, and excellent character performance." —Michael Thornton, *Sunday Express*

- "What could have been simply a money-making gimmick turns out as nimble entertainment in its own right. It's offbeat—and on the beat. It's a winner." —Dick Richards, *Daily Mirror*

- "The film is mad, mad and crazy . . . the Liverpool string quartet collectively achieves stardom in their maiden cinematic effort." —Al Finestone, *Hollywood Reporter*

- "The Beatles . . . have a neat sense of knockabout comedy timing that places them somewhere between the three Marx Brothers and the Three Stooges. Their singing style may not be for all ears, but their fun at doing it is infectious." —Arthur Knight, *Saturday Review*

- "It is, indeed, superb direction that helps to make the Beatles' film the rapid-fire, rollicking, good-humored and sophisticated spoof that it is . . . a subtle satire on the Beatle craze . . . [and] a joyous reminder of the sort of fun the Marx Brothers used to spread, done up in the cluttered climate of the television age." —Bosley Crowther, *New York Times*

- "A truly fresh, lively length of film." —*Newsweek*

The film was a worldwide box office smash, breaking old records and setting a few new ones. It eventually grossed approximately $22 million, $11 million of which was returned to United Artists to be divided among the studio, the Beatles, and Walter Shenson. In the wake of this massive success, Shenson gave Richard Lester 1 percent of the film's profits to thank him for his contribution to the picture.

The movie received two Academy Award nominations: Best Story and Screenplay— Written Directly for the Screen (Alun Owen) and Best Scoring of Music—Adaptation or Treatment (George Martin). It also received a BAFTA nomination for Most Promising Newcomer to Leading Film Roles (the Beatles) and a Grammy nomination for Best Original Score Written for a Motion Picture or Television Show (John Lennon and Paul McCartney). The Beatles won a Grammy for Best Vocal Performance for "A Hard Day's Night" (along with another for Best New Artist).

After completing its theatrical run, *A Hard Day's Night* made its television debut on NBC in October 1967 and continued to play in revival houses throughout the 1960s and 1970s. In accordance with the terms of their original contract, Walter Shenson acquired all rights to the picture from United Artists in 1979 and then made a deal with Universal Pictures to re-release it. Looking to attract audiences with the promise of something new, Shenson decided to make use of "I'll Cry Instead" (as the tune had been composed specifically for the movie, the screen rights belonged to the producer). There was no place for it in the body of the film, so Shenson created a new prologue in which the song would accompany a montage of more than three hundred

behind-the-scenes photos and publicity stills from the production. Lester (and later many critics) objected, feeling that
the prologue ruined the impact of the title song's opening
chord, but Shenson went ahead anyway. He also had the
movie's soundtrack remixed in Dolby stereo. The re-release
was originally scheduled for early 1981, but following John
Lennon's assassination in December 1980, Shenson pushed it
back to 1982 so that it wouldn't appear that he was attempting to profit from the tragedy.

The movie (in its 1982 version) first appeared on VHS
and laser disc in the late 1980s. In the early 1990s it was issued on CD-ROM; it made its DVD debut in 1997. In 1999,
a poll conducted by the British Film Institute named *A Hard
Day's Night* one of the greatest British films of the twentieth
century. That same year, Walter Shenson partnered with
Miramax for another re-release. The prologue was removed,
the negative (which had deteriorated badly) was restored,
and a new digital sound mix was created. This edition was
released theatrically in 2000, on DVD in 2002, and on Blu-
Ray in 2009.

The soundtrack album has also had a robust afterlife.
The British and American LPs were both reprinted numerous times in the 1960s and 1970s and both also issued on
cassette and eight-track tape. In the late 1970s, EMI bought
United Artists Records and assumed control of its library,

including ownership of the UAR version of the *A Hard Day's Night* soundtrack album. The American version was retired (along with *Something New*) and the Parlophone incarnation is now the only one available. The mono version of the Parlophone album was issued on CD in 1987, and a remastered CD was released in 2009 in both mono and stereo. In 2010 the album became available for the first time as an MP3 download.

A Hard Day's Night has had a major impact on the popular culture.

To begin with, its worldwide box office and record chart success cemented the Beatles' position as the biggest entertainment act on the planet. The positive critical response made them one of the most significant, a status they maintain to this day.

The film also propelled Richard Lester into the front ranks of international filmmakers. As one of the major directors of the 1960s and 1970s, he used the impressive talent he displayed in *A Hard Day's Night* to tackle a series of diverse and ambitious projects including: *The Knack. . . and How to Get It*, *A Funny Thing Happened on the Way to the Forum*, *How I Won the War*, *Petulia*, *The Bed Sitting Room*, *The Three Musketeers*, *Juggernaut*, *The Four Musketeers*, *Robin and Marian*, *Cuba*, *Superman II*, and *Superman III*.

The success of *A Hard Day's Night* generated more Beatles movies. In 1965, the band reunited with Lester and Walter Shenson to make *Help!*, a pop-art romp in which the lads are pursued by a wacky Eastern cult that is after one of Ringo's rings, which, as it turns out, is a sacred relic. The film featured seven new songs—including classics such as "Ticket to Ride," "You've Got to Hide Your Love Away," and, of course, "Help!"—and equaled the box office success of its predecessor.

Walter Shenson attempted to develop a third film for the group. Adaptations of *The Three Musketeers* and Richard Condon's *A Talent for Loving*, as well as an original screenplay coauthored by playwright Joe Orton called *Up Against It*, were considered, but never came to fruition. A few years later, Denis O'Dell tried to mount a screen version of *The Lord of the Rings* starring the boys, but the project fell apart after its intended director, Stanley Kubrick, backed out. In 1967, the band devised and directed a one-hour musical fantasy for British television called *Magical Mystery Tour*, which received poor reviews but generated a best-selling EP. *Yellow Submarine*, an animated musical based on a song from *Revolver*, was released in 1968. The film was produced by George Dunning and Al Brodax, the creative team responsible for *The Beatles*, a Saturday-morning cartoon series modeled after *A Hard Day's Night* that ran on America's ABC network from 1965 to 1969. The Beatles had no involvement in the cartoon show and were only peripherally involved in *Yellow Submarine*, contributing a few new songs and making a brief cameo appearance at the end. The band finally satisfied its three-film contract with United Artists with *Let It Be*, a documentary about the making of the group's last album.

The boys were also involved in a number of cinematic projects as individuals: John appeared in Richard Lester's 1967 war film spoof *How I Won the War* and Ringo acted in several movies, including *Candy*, *The Magic Christian*, and *Caveman*; George started Handmade Films (*Monty Python's Life of Brian*, *Time Bandits*), which became one of the most prominent independent film companies of the 1980s; Paul wrote and starred in 1984's *Give My Regards to Broad Street* and reunited with Richard Lester to make 1991's *Get Back*, a concert picture about McCartney's 1989 concert tour.

In 1991, *The Beatles: The First U.S. Visit* was issued on home video. The film, which some reviewers called "the real *A Hard Day's Night*" for its behind-the-scenes look at the band on the road, was a black-and-white documentary about the group's 1964 visit to America. Alternate edits of the footage, shot by renowned cinema verité filmmakers Albert and David Maysles, had previously appeared on England's Granada TV in February 1964 as *Yeah! Yeah! Yeah! The Beatles in New York* and on CBS in November 1964 as *The*

Beatles in America. In 1995, Walter Shenson brought everything full circle when he executive produced *You Can't Do That!: The Making of* A Hard Day's Night. Hosted by Phil Collins, who was an extra in the concert scene, the documentary premiered in the United States on PBS stations and was later released on DVD.

Finally, *A Hard Day's Night* has had a profound effect on the way rock 'n' roll is presented on film. First, it put an end to the traditional pop musical. The last sincere stabs at the genre—Cliff Richard's *Finders Keepers* and *Catch Us If You Can* (released in the United States as *Having a Wild Weekend*), starring the Dave Clark Five—both seemed hopelessly dated and stale after the Beatles' film and failed to meet expectations at the box office. Most of the pop musicals that came after *A Hard Day's Night* tried to imitate it and fell flat, none more spectacularly than a pair of films starring the charm-free members of Herman's Hermits: *Hold On* and *Mrs. Brown You've Got a Lovely Daughter,* whose forced wackiness and awkward attempts at Lester-like surrealist comedy were painfully leaden. Television attempted to ape the Beatles with *The Monkees*, a sitcom about a goofy four-man rock band (which some critics derisively dubbed the Pre-Fab Four) that traded *Night's* wit and satire for slapstick and silliness. The show was amiable enough, but *Head*—the band's feature debut—pushed the pop musical into a sour, drug-induced trippiness that proved to be the final nail in the genre's coffin.

In the 1970s, pop musicals were largely supplanted by concert films: documentaries about rockers that captured performances using techniques—including extreme close-ups of the musicians playing their instruments, handheld cameras swirling around singers, and lots and lots of lens flares—clearly inspired by Richard Lester's approach to filming the Beatles at work. By the 1980s, concert films had given way to music videos, a medium whose core aesthetic—non-linear, often surreal narrative conveyed through a steady steam of eye-popping visuals and frenetic editing—owes so much to the "I Should Have Known Better" and "escape" scenes in *A Hard Day's Night* that MTV once presented Lester with a certificate heralding him as the father of the music video, prompting the director to jokingly demand a blood test.

EPILOGUE: AND IN THE END

The release of *A Hard Day's Night* was the high point of Beatlemania. In the years that followed, the boys began to grow weary of the grueling, high-pressured schedule and fishbowl existence that the film depicted so well. Eventually they stopped touring and concentrated solely on studio work. In the process, they left Merseybeat behind and began producing material that was much more abstract and experimental. Internal conflicts and external controversies also took their toll, and in 1970 the band members decided to go their separate ways. The Beatles are no more, but their music lives on, and thanks to Richard Lester, Walter Shenson, and Alun Owen, so does a wonderful piece of celluloid that perfectly captured that happy moment so long ago, when four young men came from out of nowhere to captivate the world with their boundless energy, their buoyant spirit, and their brilliant music.

A Walter Shenson Production
A Hard Day's Night

Directed by . . . . Richard Lester

Produced by . . . . Walter Shenson

Original Screenplay by . . . . Alun Owen

Associate Producer . . . . Denis O'Dell

Director of Photography . . . . Gilbert Taylor, BSC

Musical Director . . . . George Martin

Songs by . . . . John Lennon and Paul McCartney

Art Director . . . . Ray Simm

Editor . . . . John Jympson

Assistant Director. . . . . John D. Merriman

Camera Operator . . . . Derek V. Browne

Costume Designer . . . . Julie Harris

Beatles' Wardrobe. . . . . Dougie Millings and Son

Makeup . . . . John O'Gorman

Hairdressing . . . . Betty Glasow

Continuity . . . . Rita Davison

Titles Design . . . . Robert Freeman

Sound Recording . . . . H. L. Bird and Stephen Dalby

Sound Editor. . . . . Gordon Daniel

Assistant Editor. Pamela Tomling

THE CAST

John . . . . John Lennon

Paul. . . . . Paul McCartney

George . . . . George Harrison

Ringo . . . . Ringo Starr

Grandfather. . . . . Wilfrid Brambell

Norm . . . . Norman Rossington

Shake . . . . John Junkin

TV Director. . . . . Victor Spinetti

Millie . . . . Anna Quayle

Police Inspector . . . . Deryck Guyler

Man on Train . . . . Richard Vernon

Hotel Waiter . . . . Eddie Malin

TV Floor Manager . . . . Robin Ray

TV Choreographer. Lionel Blair

Secretary . . . . Alison Seebohm
Young Boy . . . . David Jaxon

Made at Twickenham Studios, London, England
Released through United Artists

SOUNDTRACK ALBUMS

The songs from *A Hard Day's Night* were released on four different albums: the United Artists Records soundtrack issued in the United States; the Parlophone soundtrack released in the rest of the world; Capitol's *Something New*, which was issued in the United States, on American armed forces bases worldwide, and in Germany; and UAR's *A Hard Day's Night: Instrumental Versions of the Motion Picture Score*, which was released in the United States. Following EMI's acquisition of United Artists Records in 1979, both the UAR version of the soundtrack and *Something New* were retired. The Parlophone version now stands as the definitive version of the *A Hard Day's Night* soundtrack.

The first three albums were released on LP and tape in several editions throughout the 1960s and 1970s (*Instrumental* was only released once on LP; as it did poorly, no other editions were ever issued). The Parlophone version has also been released on CD and MP3 in different configurations. The following listings are those of the original LPs:

A Hard Day's Night: *Original Motion Picture Soundtrack* (1964)

Album Produced by George Martin

Songs Written by John Lennon and Paul McCartney

Songs Performed by the Beatles

Instrumental Songs Performed by George Martin and His Orchestra

Released by United Artists Records

SIDE ONE

"A Hard Day's Night"

"Tell Me Why"

"I'll Cry Instead"

"I Should Have Known Better" [Instrumental]

"I'm Happy Just to Dance with You"

"And I Love Her" [Instrumental]

SIDE TWO

"I Should Have Known Better"

"If I Fell"

"And I Love Her"
"Ringo's Theme" (This Boy) [Instrumental]
"Can't Buy Me Love"
"A Hard Day's Night" [Instrumental]

A Hard Day's Night (1964)

Album Produced by George Martin
Songs Written by John Lennon and Paul McCartney
Performed by the Beatles
Released by Parlophone Records

SIDE ONE

"A Hard Day's Night"
"I Should Have Known Better"
"If I Fell"
"I'm Happy Just to Dance with You"
"And I Love Her"
"Tell Me Why"
"Can't Buy Me Love"

SIDE TWO

"Any Time at All"
"I'll Cry Instead"
"Things We Said Today"
"When I Get Home"

"You Can't Do That"
"I'll Be Back"

Something New (1964)

Album Produced by George Martin
Songs Written by John Lennon and Paul McCartney,
except as noted
Songs Performed by the Beatles
Released by Capitol Records

SIDE ONE

"I'll Cry Instead"
"Things We Said Today"
"Any Time at All"
"When I Get Home"
"Slow Down" (Larry Williams)
"Matchbox" (Carl Perkins)

SIDE TWO

"Tell Me Why"
"And I Love Her"
"I'm Happy Just to Dance with You"
"If I Fell"
"Komm Gib Mir Deine Hand" (Lennon/McCartney/
Nicholas/Heller)

A Hard Day's Night: *Instrumental Versions of the Motion Picture Score* (1964)

Album Produced by George Martin
Songs Written by John Lennon and Paul McCartney
Songs Performed by George Martin and His Orchestra
Released by United Artists Records

SIDE ONE

"I Should Have Known Better"
"Tell Me Why"
"I'm Happy Just to Dance with You"
"If I Fell"
"And I Love Her"
"Ringo's Theme" (This Boy)

SIDE TWO

"A Hard Day's Night"
"I'll Cry Instead"
"I Want to Hold Your Hand"
"All My Loving"
"She Loves You"
"Can't Buy Me Love"
"Don't Bother Me"

ACKNOWLEDGMENTS

I would like to thank David V. Picker for his invaluable contributions to this book.

Thanks also to my agent, June Clark of FinePrint Literary Management, Barry Monush, the series editor, and John Cerullo and Marybeth Keating at Hal Leonard Performing Arts Publishing Group, for their tremendous support..

For their technical facilitation and assistance, I would like to thank Andrew Morton, M. F. Harmon, and Raymond J. Morton Sr. I would also like to acknowledge the staff of the Margaret E. Herrick Library at the Academy of Motion Picture Arts and Sciences for their help and assistance.

On a personal note, I would like to thank the members of my family for their continuing love and support: Raymond J. Morton Sr. and Rita K. Morton; Kathy, Dan, and Caitlin Hoey; Nancy, Kate, Maddie, and Carrie Lutian; Rich and

Kendra Morton; William Morton; Ken Morton; Claire and Derek Masterbone; Andrew Morton; Tom, Lindsey, Erin, and Jack Morton.

Thanks too to my wonderful friends: Maggie Morrisette; M. F. and Linda Harmon; Carmen and Dan Apodaca; Terri Barbagallo; Dharmesh Chauhan; Gina, David, and Eva Fénard; Brian Finn; Faith Ginsberg; Tara, Kurt, Mia, and Mattius Johnson; Richard H. Kline; Janet McKenney and Holly Valero, Alison, John, and Bethany Aurora Nelson; Tim Partridge; Gary Pearle; Donna and Joe Romeo; Stephen Tropiano and Steven Ginsberg.

Finally, I would like to thank Ana Maria Apodaca for letting me hold her hand.

BIBLIOGRAPHY

Books

Balio, Tino. *United Artists: The Company That Changed the Film Industry*. Madison: University of Wisconsin Press, 1987.

Brown, Peter, and Steven Gaines. *The Love You Make: An Insider's Story of The Beatles*. New York: Signet, 1983.

Di Franco, J. Philip, ed. *The Beatles in Richard Lester's* A Hard Day's Night: *A Complete Pictorial Record of the Movie*. New York: Penguin, 1978.

Glynn, Stephen. *Turner Classic Movies British Film Guide:* A Hard Day's Night. London: I. B. Tauris, 2005.

Hertsgaard, Mark. *A Day in the Life: The Music and Artistry of the Beatles*. New York: Delacorte Press, 1995.

Lennon, John. *In His Own Write & A Spaniard in the Works*. New York: Signet, 1981.

Lewisohn, Mark. *The Complete Beatles Chronicle*. London: Hamlyn, 2000.

Martin, George with Jeremy Hornsby. *All You Need Is Ears*. New York: St. Martin's Press, 1994.

Norman, Philip. *Shout! The Beatles in Their Generation*. New York: Fireside, 1996.

———. *John Lennon: The Life*. New York: Harper Collins, 2008.

O'Dell, Denis, with Bob Neaverson. *At the Apple's Core: The Beatles from the Inside*. London: Peter Owen, 2002.

Orton, Joe. *Head to Toe: A Novel & Up Against It: A Screenplay for the Beatles*. New York: Da Capo Press, 1998.

Pritchard, David, and Alan Lysaght. *The Beatles: An Oral History*. New York: Hyperion, 1998.

Rolston, Lorraine, and Andy Murray. *The Ultimate Film Guides: A Hard Day's Night*. London: York Press, 2001.

Sheff, David, and G. Barry Golson, eds. *The Playboy Interviews with John Lennon and Yoko Ono*. New York: Playboy Press, 1981.

Sinyard, Neil. *The Films of Richard Lester*. Beckenham: Croom Helm, 1985.

Soderbergh, Steven, and Richard Lester. *Getting Away with It Or: The Further Adventures of the Luckiest Bastard You Ever Saw*. London: Faber and Faber, 1999.

Spitz, Bob. *The Beatles: The Biography*. New York: Little, Brown, 2005.

Walker, Alexander. *Hollywood U.K.* New York: Stein and Day, 1974.

Yule, Andrew. *The Man Who "Framed" the Beatles: A Biography of Richard Lester*. New York: Donald I. Fine, 1994.

Articles

"Biggest Music Promotion Backs Beatles Feature." *Motion Picture Exhibitor*, July 8, 1964.

Champlin, Charles. "Beatlemania Revisited." *Los Angeles Times*, April 5, 1974.

———. "A Day in the Life—When Their World Was Young." *Los Angeles Times*, November 20, 1982, Calendar 1, 8.

Doherty, Thomas. "The Beatles Invasion." *American Movie Classics Magazine* (Sept. 1966):4-6.

Edward, Mark. "Say You Want a Revolution." *Sunday Times*, April 8, 2001, Magazine 14.

Friendly, David T. "David Picker: Out of the Cold, Into Columbia." *Los Angeles Times*, December 4, 1986.

Kozinn, Allan. "From the Beatles' Moment of Glory." *New York Times*, November 26, 2000, Arts & Leisure 1, 24.

McCarthy, Todd. "Shenson's New *Hard Day's Night* Rehash Shops Post-UA Distrib Tie." *Variety*, July 22, 1981, 7, 30.

Pritchard, David, and Alan Lysaght. "The Fab Four Frolic Again." *Box Office* (Feb. 1999):24-26.

Rense, Rip. "He's Bringing Back Beatles Through Film." *Los Angeles Herald-Examiner*, May 18, 1982, C1, C4.

Sragow, Michael. "*A Hard Day's Night* Dawns Again." *Rolling Stone* (June 24, 1982).

Williams, David E. "Gilbert Taylor, BSC is Given the Spotlight with the ASC's International Achievement Award." *American Cinematographer* (Feb. 2006).

Internet

Burgess, Steve. "Richard Lester: A hard day's life." *Salon.com*, June 26, 1999. http://www.salon.com/people/rewind/1999/06/26/lester.

Calkin, Graham. "A Hard Day's Night." *Graham Calkin's Beatles Pages*, 2001. http://www.jpgr.co.uk/pcs3058.html.

Harry, Bill. "A Hard Day's Night." *Sixties City: Bill Harry's Sixties*. http://www.sixtiescity.com/Mbeat/mbfilms71.htm.

Hook, Chris. "The Hard Day's Night Chord: Rock's Holy Grail." *Everything 2*. http://everything2.com/index.pl?node_id=1718612.

James, Gary. "Gary James' Interview with Beatles' Publicist Jerry Pam." *Classic Bands*.com. http://www.classicbands.com/JerryPamInterview.html.

———. "Walter Shenson Interview: Remembering the Beatles." www.*Famous Interview.com.* http://www.famousinterview.ca/interviews/walter_shenson.htm.

Michaels, Ken. "An Interview with John Junkin." 2006. http://abbeyrd.best.vwh.net/johnjunkin.html.

Phipps, Keith. "Richard Lester." *A.V. Club*, November 7, 2007. http://www.avclub.com/articles/richard-lester,14167/.

Rybaczewski, Dave. "A Hard Day's Night Soundtrack History." *Beatles Music History*. http://www.beatlesebooks.com/hard-days-night-soundtrack.

Spizer, Bruce. "A Hard Day's Night United Artists Releases." www.beatle.net. http://www.beatle.net/articles/ahdn.html.

Documentaries

"Give Me Everything: A Companion Anthology." *A Hard Day's Night*—Miramax Collector's Series DVD. Buena Vista Home Entertainment, 2002.

Smeaton, Bob, Geoff Wonfor, and Kevin Godley (directors). *The Beatles Anthology* (DVD version). Apple/EMI Distribution, 2003.

You Can't Do That!: The Making of a Hard Day's Night. Apple/MPI Home Video, 1995.

Screenplay

Owen, Alun. *A Hard Day's Night.* Second draft, 1964.

Other

A Hard Day's Night Press Notes, 2000.

INDEX